Advance praise for
The Lac-Mégantic Rail Disaster

"Bruce Campbell has carried out meticulous research in many fields to piece together the whole story of a catastrophe-in-the-making, and his findings, as reported in this book, will be of interest to readers who value human life, intact communities, and a safe environment. Much more than a research report, the book is a dramatic read, with no letup in the action from start to finish."

— Harry Gow, former criminology teacher, University of Ottawa, President Emeritus of Transport Action Canada and Chair of the Board of the Public Interest Advocacy Centre

"Bruce Campbell has made a superb contribution. His vivid account of the events at Lac-Mégantic reveal a deep empathy for the victims. He accords them the highest respect possible by avoiding sentiment and explaining why it all happened. He puts the tragedy in its economic and political context. He shows how the internalization of neoliberalism by our political elites has made it too easy for predators. Deregulation to satisfy the avaricious heedless of human welfare, is carefully documented. The associated disciplining of bureaucrats and the corruption of corruptible regulators is brought out with precision. Campbell proves that the Lac-Mégantic disaster was a designed event, not an accident. The law's failure to punish the truly guilty endorses his point. This is a "must read' for all, but especially for those of us who want to believe that our political and legal institutions are there to protect us, rather than private profiteers."

— Harry Glasbeek, Professor Emeritus and Senior Scholar, Osgoode Hall Law School and author of *Capitalism: A Crime Story*

The
Lac-Mégantic
Rail Disaster

PUBLIC BETRAYAL,
JUSTICE DENIED

To Bill

BRUCE CAMPBELL

James Lorimer & Company Ltd., Publishers
Toronto

James Lorimer & Company Ltd., Publishers acknowledges funding support from the Ontario Arts Council (OAC), an agency of the Government of Ontario. We acknowledge the support of the Canada Council for the Arts, which last year invested $153 million to bring the arts to Canadians throughout the country. This project has been made possible in part by the Government of Canada and with the support of the Ontario Media Development Corporation.

Cover design: Tyler Cleroux

Cover image: Archive/Agence QMI

Library and Archives Canada Cataloguing in Publication

Campbell, Bruce, 1948-, author
    The Lac-Mégantic rail disaster : public betrayal, justice denied / Bruce Campbell.

Includes bibliographical references and index.
Issued in print and electronic formats.
ISBN 978-1-4594-1341-2 (hardcover).--ISBN 978-1-4594-1342-9 (EPUB)

    1. Lac-Mégantic Derailment, Lac-Mégantic, Québec, 2013. 2. Railroad accidents--Investigation--Québec (Province)--Lac-Mégantic. I. Title.

HE1783.C3C36 2018   363.12'20971469   C2018-904024-6
                                                     C2018-904025-4

James Lorimer & Company Ltd., Publishers
117 Peter Street, Suite 304
Toronto, ON, Canada
M5V 0M3
www.lorimer.ca

Printed and bound in Canada.

To the forty-seven victims who perished in this senseless tragedy;
To their twenty-seven orphaned children, to their families and friends;
and to the people of Lac-Mégantic;
To all who are fighting to uncover the whole truth
behind the disaster;
To all who are fighting to keep its memory alive;
To all who are fighting to prevent history from repeating itself.

CONTENTS

MAPS

MAP 1: TRAIN ROUTE

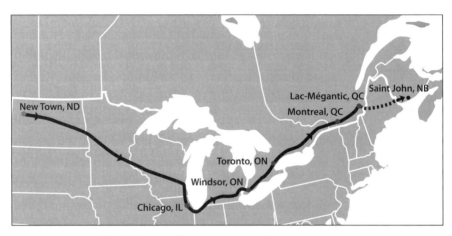

Source: Transportation Safety Board report

MAP 2: EASTERN PORTION

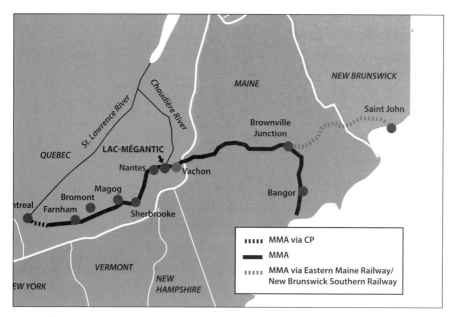

Source: Transportation Safety Board report

MAP 3: DISASTER SITE

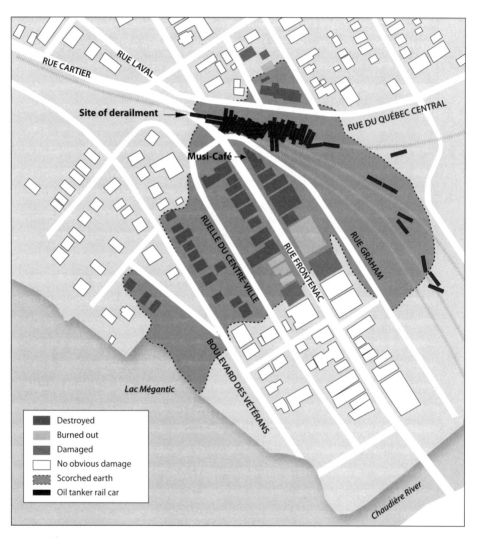

Source: The *Toronto Star*

INTRODUCTION

At 11 p.m. on July 5, 2013, a 10,290-ton train is parked on the main track on top of a hill in Nantes, a village in the southeast corner of Quebec. The night is warm, the air still. The stars shine brightly in a cloudless sky.

The train, hauling seventy-two tank cars loaded with high-volatility crude oil, belongs to Montreal, Maine and Atlantic Railway, a small, American-owned company. But the cargo began its journey under the charge of a much larger company, Canadian Pacific Railway (CP).

CP hauled the oil from New Town, situated atop the Bakken shale formation in North Dakota, some four thousand kilometres to Montreal. After winding its way through cities and towns in Minnesota, Illinois and Michigan, the train entered Canada at Windsor. In Ontario, it travelled through numerous communities, including downtown Toronto, before arriving in Montreal on July 4. The chain of tank cars was transported to Farnham and handed off to Montreal, Maine and Atlantic Railway early the next morning for the two-hundred-kilometre trip to Nantes.

The railway's owner, seventy-five-year-old Ed Burkhardt, is a lifelong railroad entrepreneur with a stable of freight companies in the United

States and Europe. Burkhardt is likely asleep at home in Kenilworth, a Chicago suburb, secure in the knowledge that years of cost-cutting, in concert with the lucrative new revenue stream of Bakken shale oil, bodes well financially.

The train is scheduled to continue the next day on its journey through Maine to its final destination: the Irving Oil refinery in Saint John, New Brunswick. The crew consists of one person: engineer Tom Harding. He's worried by how the lead locomotive has been smoking, sputtering and spewing oil on the ten-and-a-half hour trip from Farnham, just south of Montreal. He calls the rail traffic controller at company headquarters in Hermon, a suburb of Bangor, Maine.

The rail traffic controller tells him not to worry. "Just leave it, Tom. It will settle down. The American crew will assess the problem in the morning."

An exhausted Harding sets some handbrakes. Following company procedure, he leaves the lead locomotive running so its air brakes can also be applied.

Eleven kilometres away lies Lac-Mégantic, a town of nearly six thousand nestled in a basin beside the lake of the same name. Surrounded by rolling countryside, the town is a popular destination for hikers, cyclists, cottagers, swimmers and amateur astronomers attracted by the observatory on nearby Mount Mégantic.

The town is humming on this balmy summer night. Boats line the marina. The main street is crowded. A popular nightspot, the Musi-Café, is crammed with people. A band that reunites two popular Quebec musicians has the dance floor packed. The club is a mere fifteen metres from where the train track curves sharply in the centre of town.

At 11:30 p.m., Harding leaves the train — unattended, in accordance with company policy. It was the last time he would see his train intact.

NOT ONE DISASTER, BUT THREE

This book is the story of the disasters that followed after Tom Harding parked the oil train, and how they came to pass.

I say disasters in the plural because the inferno that consumed the town core that summer night was the calamity that triggered a series of subsequent tragedies in Lac-Mégantic. With forty-seven people dead, six million litres of oil spilled and the centre of a historic town charred, it was the largest disaster on Canadian soil since the 1917 Halifax Explosion.

People across North America watching on TV or YouTube asked themselves: How could the government let this happen? What if the derailment had happened not in a town of six thousand but in a metropolis like Toronto or Montreal?

As ensuing chapters will show, the disaster was the direct result of decisions made by companies, and by governments that are supposed to protect the public. A long pattern of loosening safety standards in the name of deregulation and cutting red tape made the catastrophe in Lac-Mégantic possible.

Canadians were wrong to think their safety was being safeguarded, and they were also wrong to think things would change after the heart of a community was immolated. Many of the conditions that led to the disaster are still in place. Deregulation, along with its neoliberal sibling policies, was responsible for the inferno, but the inferno barely singed deregulation.

What's more, those responsible were not held accountable.

Another disaster of Lac-Mégantic was the exploitation of the victims' families. National media interest faded in the months following the disaster, but a new tragedy was arriving in the form of ambulance chasers and disaster capitalists.

These shocking tales — cascading tragedies — have not been fully told before now.

RAILWAY NATION, RAILWAY TOWN

The Lac-Mégantic story is a very Canadian one. Railways built Canada, gaining along the way enough power to hijack and corrupt governments, as in the infamous Pacific Scandal that ended the government of John A. Macdonald in 1873. Lac-Mégantic, like many of the country's towns and cities, owes its existence to the railway.

The town was founded in 1884 by CP as it was building the eastern leg of its transcontinental line. The line was operational in 1889, running from Lac-Mégantic through Maine (via its subsidiary, the International Railway of Maine) to Saint John, New Brunswick.

The completion of this last leg made CP the first truly transcontinental railway company in Canada, enabling transatlantic cargo and passenger services to continue year-round, unencumbered by sea ice in the Gulf of St. Lawrence that closed the port of Montreal during the winter months.

Lac-Mégantic is situated at the southeast corner of Quebec on the edge of the Appalachian Mountains, close to the border with Maine. The Chaudière River, flowing north to the St. Lawrence River, divides the town into two parishes: Notre-Dame-de-Fatima to the south and St. Agnès to the north.

J.H. Pope, entrepreneur and local member of Parliament, built a railway between Sherbrooke and Lac-Mégantic in 1878. Prime Minister John A. Macdonald came to town to inaugurate the new line. CP bought it a few years later and absorbed it into its transcontinental railway network.

Situated on a vital transport axis, Lac-Mégantic became an important hub, linking the Maritimes to the rest of Canada. Apart from the transcontinental and Sherbrooke lines, it was also a junction for the Quebec Central Railway, connecting points north to Quebec City and southeast to Maine and beyond. CP located equipment repair shops in the town as well as a large switching and storage yard. CP built Lac-Mégantic's distinctive railway station, which still stands, in 1926.

In April 1918, a runaway CP train from Nantes collided with another train at the curve in front of the St. Agnès church in the heart of town — the exact spot where the tragedy of 2013 occurred. Two people were killed.

During the economic boom following the Second World War, the town's population grew to 7,500 by 1960. Thereafter it began to diminish due to a falling birth rate, departing youth and major shifts in its economy. By the mid-1980s it had shrunk to its current size of about six thousand residents. Its importance as a railway town declined with the rise of road transportation and the replacement of the steam engine with lower-maintenance diesel locomotives. CP closed its repair shop and Quebec Central Railway abandoned its line through Lac-Mégantic in the mid-1990s. It was eventually sold to a local resident; it went out of business in 2006.

The CP passenger train, which ran through Lac-Mégantic to Maine and then on to Halifax, was taken over by the publicly owned Via Rail in 1978. Due largely to Liberal government pressure, the service was eliminated in 1997 in favour of the Quebec South Shore–Northern New Brunswick route owned by the Canadian National Railway (CN). The decision was justified on the grounds that the line, by then operated by the US-owned Canadian American Railroad, would not be maintained to Via's standards.

As with many small and mid-sized communities across Quebec and Ontario, Lac-Mégantic's manufacturing sector was a casualty of globalization in the 1980s and 1990s. Food-processing plants closed, as did sawmills. The clothing sector, including the makers of Wonderbra, which employed many women, shut down, relocating to low-wage jurisdictions abroad. The decline of the railway, forestry and manufacturing sectors was somewhat offset by the growth of both tourism and Lac-Mégantic's role as a regional administrative centre for government. But like many Canadian towns and cities, Lac-Mégantic had been left behind by history, diminished in numbers, with few prospects for growth, its economy and public finances vulnerable.

Today the town's principal industries — forest products, granite and agriculture — are all dependent on the railway. The railway is vital to the town's manufacturers, which include particleboard producer Tafisa, a subsidiary of the Portuguese-owned giant Sonae Indústria; a branch of Masonite International that makes interior doors; and office furniture specialist Bestar.

The town, like so many small Canadian places, is tightly knit. "Everyone knows each other. Information spreads more by word of mouth than TV or radio," says resident Gilles Fluet. "People do not go through Lac-Mégantic on the way to somewhere else. They go to Lac-Mégantic as their final destination."

CHAPTER 1

The Liberators

The roots of the Lac-Mégantic disaster stretch back to 1984, the year Brian Mulroney and the Progressive Conservative party came to power, intent on bringing Canada into the new political project — neoliberalism — that was sweeping the world.

The project was designed to change the rules of the game in Western economies: to transform relations of power between the state and corporations, between corporations and workers and between the state and its citizens. The techniques included deregulation, privatization, monetary and fiscal austerity and trade and investment liberalization.

Neoliberalism's narrative, described by US President Ronald Reagan as "unleashing the magic of the marketplace," held that governments should do as little as possible and let corporations get on with their essential role as job and wealth creators. Government's primary economic role was to uphold and enforce market disciplines.

The 1980–81 global recession, the worst since the Great Depression, wreaked havoc on an already weakened international economic order. The moment gave project advocates — economic thinkers led by

Milton Friedman; their political standard-bearers, Reagan and Margaret Thatcher; and corporate-financed lobby groups and think tanks — the crisis moment they were waiting for to impose their solutions on a world adrift. Canada had been slow to embrace the new paradigm, but that was about to change.

Mulroney himself came from the sphere of American big business. Prior to becoming Progressive Conservative leader in 1983, he was president of the Labrador-based Iron Ore Company of Canada, a branch plant of an American giant, Hanna Mining, which owned Quebec North Shore and Labrador Railway.

No policy heavyweight, Mulroney took his cues from the newly formed Business Council on National Issues, a lobby group created by Tom d'Aquino, a former adviser to Pierre Trudeau. Comprised of the CEOs of the 150 largest corporations in Canada, the Business Council on National Issues sought to influence government at the highest level, aided by business-funded think tanks such as the C.D. Howe Institute and the Fraser Institute.

The Mulroney government immediately got to work on an ambitious program of deregulation and privatization. It loosened foreign investment restrictions; killed the National Energy Program, with which Trudeau tried to change the balance of power between Ottawa and Big Oil; deregulated the petroleum industry; and later partially privatized the Trudeau-created state oil company, Petro-Canada, and prepared the groundwork for the privatization of CN.

Deregulation was so central to the new government that Mulroney put his deputy prime minister, Erik Nielsen, on the job the day after the new government was elected. Nielsen was to head a task force whose goal was to root out inefficiency and red tape, and to reduce the size of government and the scope of its intervention in the economy. Regulations were identified as a hidden cost and a burden to business.

The Nielsen task force produced a report on regulatory reform that, to the surprise of no one, concluded that Canada was indeed over-regulated. In short order, a Ministry of State for Privatization and

Regulatory Affairs was created. Successive government budgets cut regulatory resources and personnel.

"Deregulation," however, can mean different things. When the United States began to deregulate its railways in the early 1980s with the *Staggers Rail Act*, it confined changes to economic activities. The rules around ownership and rate structures were loosened, but it did not deregulate railway safety. Transport regulators retained their prescriptive power to order companies to implement safety measures.

The Canadian government under Mulroney followed suit on the economic dimension of deregulation, but it deregulated rail safety as well. The *Railway Safety Act* was introduced in 1985. The *Act*, which came into force in 1988, began to devolve the management of safety to the railway companies themselves.

But an act of Parliament in itself would not be sufficient — the deregulation of rail safety would require a reorganization of institutions governing the transportation sector.

Nielsen resigned from Parliament in 1987 and was appointed chair of the Canadian Transport Commission, the independent regulator overseeing all modes of transportation. The commission was dismantled and its functions divided up.

Safety-regulations responsibilities were brought inside Transport Canada itself, giving it the dual mandate of safety regulator and economic promoter. Within Transport Canada were located two directorates: Rail Safety and Transport of Dangerous Goods. The Transportation Safety Board was created as an independent agency to investigate accidents and make recommendations to Transport Canada.

The National Transportation Agency was also created as an independent body. Its name was changed to the Canadian Transportation Agency in 1996. It is responsible for economic regulations: issuing railway operating certificates, approving new railway lines and resolving disputes with the public and with other levels of government.

The Mulroney overhaul of the transportation regulatory system included staff reductions and the gutting of the remedial powers of all three bodies — Transport Canada, the Canadian Transportation Agency and the Transportation Safety Board. They effectively check-mated Transport Canada's ability to order the railways to take specific safety measures, limiting their powers to ordering them to *stop* taking unsafe activities.

A key step in achieving this drawback of government power occurred with the 1998 *Railway Safety Act*. It included a new regime called the Canadian Rail Operating Rules.

The word "rules" is key. Transport Canada still established regulations, but their numbers were reduced and replaced by rules. Where Transport Canada inspectors previously had been able to issue "orders" telling railways what to do, now the field was governed largely by "rules" that were written, in most cases, by the companies themselves. Rules required approval from the minister, but this largely became a rubber stamp.

It was a major victory for the railways. As one former insider told me: "This is where things went astray: When you put the fox in charge of the chicken coop, you need to have someone with a pretty big gun watching the fox."

The new regime gave railways a freer hand to change all manner of time-proven procedures. During this period, for example, the caboose — integral to monitoring the condition of the railcars, road crossings, etc. and communicating with the locomotive engineer, other crew members and rail traffic controllers — was eliminated from freight trains, and crew sizes shrank from five to two.

The *Railway Safety Act*, along with the *Canada Labour Code*, dictated that employees and unions would be consulted in the rule-making process. However, under the Mulroney government a practice took hold — and persisted through subsequent administrations — of merely paying lip service to consultation. One former transportation industry insider told me: "It is all a huge sham." It was a closed-door process to which no outside groups had access.

REGULATORY CAPTURE IN RAILWAYS

That a disaster the size of Lac-Mégantic should happen in a country that ought to know a thing or two about rail safety reflects the formidable challenge of maintaining the independence of regulators. If the industry being regulated writes the rules; shapes the regulations and statutes; and many of the senior decision-makers in the department come from its own ranks and identify with its interests, the regulator has been "captured."

Regulatory capture embodies a fundamental conflict between the primary obligation of government to protect the health and safety of its citizens and the interests of corporations to maximize shareholder value.[1] If a regulator is captured — Canada's National Energy Board is a notorious example — industry removes or dilutes existing regulations it deems too expensive, shapes new regulations to suit its interests and blocks the prospect of more aggressive interventions.

Captured regulators see themselves more as a partner with industry than an independent body accountable to the public. This inappropriate cosiness stems in part from the revolving-door phenomenon: Regulators are often recruited from industry and then return to lucrative senior positions in industry after a time in government. The danger here is obvious: Managers seeking employment with industry down the road will tend to pull their punches to remain on good terms with the companies they regulate. According to a former Transport Canada insider, most senior managers in the department come from the railway industry, and many of them do not take off their railway hats after they arrive. Senior officials tend to defer to companies' expertise and economic priorities, downplaying safety considerations.

The revolving door, once installed in Ottawa under Mulroney, turned faster in subsequent governments. Harper-era Minister of Transport John Baird, after leaving politics, was appointed to a lucrative spot on the board of CP. Senior Transport Canada officials Cliff MacKay and Bill Rowat both moved from government to president and CEO of the Railway Association of Canada — the industry lobby group. Privy

Council clerk Paul Tellier was appointed CEO of CN, and was later named to the board of the Railway Association.

It's a profitable arrangement for all the companies and individuals involved. Money, indeed, governs Canada's regulatory regimes, and not just in career trajectories. The resources available to industry lobbyists — whether railways, petroleum, pharmaceuticals or other sectors — dwarf those available to public interest groups, municipalities and the like.

It's true, of course, that there is a process to weigh regulatory proposals. But industry dominates interventions in that process, both in public and in the closed-door sphere of lobbying. Public-interest group interventions are by contrast sparse and intermittent. And the general public is rarely involved in consultations.

Industry's control of information and resources enables it to commission studies by highly paid consultants or analysts at industry-supported think tanks, who then produce self-serving data presented as sound science. And even when a proposed regulation is successful, industries are able to appeal and delay its implementation. Under-resourced agencies lack their own independent body of knowledge and expertise, and are thus dependent for much of their information on the companies they regulate.

What's more, the government and public mindsets are subject to constant media bombardment by business- and industry-funded think tanks that trash regulation as a burden and a job killer.

DYSFUNCTION AT TRANSPORT CANADA
A corollary of regulatory capture is a weak and dysfunctional regulatory agency. Anaïs Valiquette L'Heureux's doctoral research at the École nationale d'administration publique in Montreal chronicled, in the years leading up to the tragedy, a fragmented organizational hierarchy. This inhibited communication among Transport Canada's regional offices and the Rail Safety and Transportation of Dangerous Goods directorates in Ottawa, between these two directorates themselves and elsewhere within headquarters.[2]

More fundamentally, L'Heureux identified an "organizational narcissism within Transport Canada. Turf wars compromised its safety mandate. Senior officials did not believe the oil-by-rail boom that would immolate Lac-Mégantic constituted a serious threat to public safety, and were thus blind to the accumulating danger signs."[3] Senior managers were more concerned with meeting the government's budget targets and protecting their own turf. Their priorities determined the distribution of budget cuts mandated by the Harper government, which fell disproportionately on sections responsible for safety. Positions were left vacant or merged. Experts were replaced by less-qualified staff.

There was a lack of trust and mutual respect between the intermediate and front-line staff, which had the technical expertise, and the decision-making level, which did not. There was a bias among senior management toward company self-regulation, and a predisposition against enforcement of existing regulations. L'Heureux's study found senior staff at Transport Canada routinely ignored company transgressions, producing frustration and demoralization among the railway inspectorate.[4]

An example comes from the experience of Jean-Pierre Gagnon, one of Canada's foremost experts on tank cars, used to transport liquids — dangerous and otherwise — by train. He was "retired" as part of the government's austerity agenda. Gagnon, a professional engineer, is scathing about senior managers' lack of understanding of the problems with conventional DOT-111 tank cars, and about their lack of concern for the Transportation Safety Board's repeated warnings that they were unsafe for carrying dangerous goods. Gagnon confirmed the high level of dysfunctionality at Transport Canada when it came to safety. The consequences for Lac-Mégantic would be dire.

Over time, Gagnon says, the technical capacity of the department shrank as staff were laid off or retired and not replaced. Gradually, the capacity to do independent analysis and evaluation diminished. According to Gagnon, senior officials in the Harper years were simply following the lead handed down from the top, namely an aversion to science and evidence getting in the way of policy priorities.

A FATAL MYTH

Canada's recent history is scarred by regulatory disasters. Although the circumstances of each disaster are unique, many share similar characteristics: vague or non-existent regulations; inadequate oversight and/ or enforcement; a weak regulator captured by an industry that is given wide scope to regulate itself.[5]

Some cases in point:

- The 1982 Ocean Ranger oil rig sinking off the coast of Newfoundland (eighty-four deaths) stemmed from a complete lack of regulation. Federal and provincial governments prioritized offshore oil exploration and development above all.[6]

- In the 1992 Westray mine explosion in Nova Scotia (twenty-six deaths), politicians in charge, attracted by the promise of jobs, were wilfully blind to the dangers inherent in building the mine. Mine operations were plagued by negligent company behaviour. Safety laws were violated, regulations not enforced and inspectors' warnings ignored.[7]

- The 2000 Walkerton water contamination outbreak (seven deaths, 2,300 people made sick) was the result of an Ontario government that starved regulatory resources and offloaded inspection responsibilities to unqualified private contractors.[8]

- The 2008 listeriosis outbreak at Maple Leaf Foods in Toronto (twenty-two deaths) was precipitated by the regulatory agency offloading on-site inspections to inadequately trained company inspectors and not requiring them to report incidences of listeria-tainted meat to the agency.[9]

After each such disaster, public confidence in government's ability to protect it is shattered, and the myth of company self-regulation is exposed. All too often, unfortunately, memory fades and lessons are forgotten. The myth gets resurrected.[10]

CHAPTER 2

Railway Makeover

Deregulation was a hallmark of the Mulroney government. But in more ways than one, that Progressive Conservative regime put its imprint on Ottawa permanently. The defeat of the PCs in the 1993 election ushered in thirteen years of Liberal government under Jean Chrétien and Paul Martin, but the deregulation agenda marched onward as if there was no regime change.

The 1995 Liberal budget included a 50 per cent reduction in Transport Canada's budget, which strangled regulatory resources, including staffing levels and research. Mulroney may have initiated the North American Free Trade Agreement (NAFTA), but the Liberals passed it virtually unchanged. They also completed the privatization of Petro-Canada.

In 1995, the Liberal government privatized CN and further deregulated passenger and freight railway operations, once more following through on its predecessor's groundwork.

It was no small change: CN and CP's historic covenant to bind the country together was being rewritten. No longer were the railways to balance profit with an obligation to the citizens of Canada — who had, after all, collectively subsidized these companies for their entire history. Now the two railways were free to sell off or simply abandon unprofitable branch lines like the one running through Lac-Mégantic. The implications went beyond the smaller communities (and the businesses) that these lines had served. Both CP and CN were given free rein to abandon lines they no longer considered profitable. For example, they ripped up their Ottawa Valley lines. As a result, trains could cross Canada only by going through populous southern Ontario.

TELLIER STARTS THE BALL ROLLING

Paul Tellier was a key player in the transformation of CN. In 1992, Mulroney appointed him CEO of CN, with a privatization brief. He was certainly qualified for the job. As deputy minister of Energy, Mines and Resources from 1982 to 1985, he had presided over the dismantling of Trudeau's National Energy Program and the initiation of Petro-Canada's privatization. Appointed clerk of the Privy Council and secretary to the cabinet in 1985, Tellier was a driving force behind the PC policy agenda.

Tellier did not disappoint Mulroney. He orchestrated the largest single public share offering by a Canadian corporation up to that point, netting $1 billion for Ottawa's treasury.

Within its first three years of privatized operation, CN's profits soared to record levels. Shareholders saw the company's stock triple, while workers saw their numbers reduced by ten thousand. Services, especially to smaller, isolated communities, were reduced. Within two years of the privatization, American investors owned the majority of CN shares. Although CN was no longer under majority Canadian ownership, its head office remained in Montreal — a fig-leaf condition of privatization.

With NAFTA entrenching free movement of goods and services, as well as investment protections and the removal of foreign ownership restrictions, Tellier embarked on an ambitious plan to convert CN from an east-west Canadian company to a North American railway stretching all the way to the Mexican border.

Tellier executed his plan largely by buying American railways. His acquisitions brought onto the stage American actors who would figure in the Lac-Mégantic tragedy.

Tellier's major American purchase, in 1998, was the Illinois Central Railroad, whose chief operating officer was the hard-driving E. Hunter Harrison. Their partnership — Harrison handling operations and Tellier managing the financial side — built CN into one of the five largest railroads on the continent, one that was now exclusively a freight operation.

In 2001, CN bought Wisconsin Central, a railway in which Edward Burkhardt, another bottom-line operator, had been a major shareholder. By now, CN had rebranded itself "North America's railroad."

Having groomed Harrison as his successor, Tellier left CN in 2002 to become CEO of Canada's top train and plane maker, Bombardier. He subsequently sat on the board of two rail-industry lobby groups, the Railway Association of Canada and the Association of American Railroads. He was also vice-chair of the Canadian Council of Chief Executives, as the Business Council on National Issues renamed itself in 2001.

The sell-off of unprofitable branch lines gave rise to a proliferation of small, mostly American-owned "short line" railways that allowed many communities and industries to retain rail access. While some of these firms were well-managed and maintained high safety standards, others operated close to the financial edge, cutting corners and increasing safety risks.

The industry's changing landscape also gave rise to consolidators who assembled a stable of railways within private holding companies. One of these was Burkhardt.

ENTER HARRISON AND BURKHARDT

Harrison and Burkhardt were cut from the same cloth. Diehard railroaders since their teens, both were legends in the industry, albeit on different scales: Burkhardt was a minor player compared to Harrison.

When Harrison joined Illinois Central in 1988, it was on the verge of bankruptcy. He transformed it into a profitable enterprise by the time it was bought by CN in 1998. As CN's COO, Harrison earned his first Railroader of the Year award from the trade publication *Railway Age* in 2002.

In his characteristic Memphis drawl — or growl — Harrison conveyed his unwavering conviction of how best to operate a railroad, a conviction that would brook no dissent. His "precision railroading" approach was simple: run fewer and longer trains, eliminate unprofitable lines, reduce the head count. The effect of the latter was to increase pressure on those remaining to work longer hours, often under increasingly unsafe conditions. Harrison's cutting of services produced such a multitude of complaints from customers that it prompted the government to launch a commission of inquiry.

Harrison ran CN with an iron fist. He was a classic disruptor who believed that shaking things up was necessary. Harrison's confrontational style was a major departure from the employer-employee relationship that had characterized the industry. The number of union grievances tripled during his tenure and the number sent to arbitration was five times the level at CP. He created a "culture of intimidation," according to one union official.

Harrison's approach to safety raised concerns with a 2007 government panel assigned to review the *Railway Safety Act.* It concluded: "there appears to be a serious disconnect between CN's stated [safety] objectives and what is occurring at employee levels." It also found that CN had been under-reporting accident statistics going back to 2002, when Harrison took over as CEO.

Harrison insisted his managers learn to be locomotive engineers, dispatchers, conductors and repair-shop workers. This training would come in handy when the union went on strike, as it did several times during his tenure. When CN workers went on strike in 2007, Harrison brought in strikebreakers from the US and used management to operate his trains. In a 2009 strike, Harrison cajoled the Harper government into introducing back-to-work legislation.

Harrison regularly invited a cross-section of "promising" employees to his hunting camp for weekend retreats — they became known as "Hunter Camps" — in which he inculcated participants with his vision of railroading. Those at odds with the program did not last; those who embraced his approach were promoted. His Hunter Camp talks were collected into a book, *How We Work and Why: Running a Precision Railroad*, which was distributed to all employees.

Under his (and Tellier's) leadership, CN's operating ratio (the ratio of expenses to revenue) fell from 89 per cent in 1995 to 61 per cent in 2006, well below that of its main competitors. Harrison retired from CN at the end of 2009.

As for Burkhardt, he may have been a legend in some quarters, but in others he was the devil incarnate. A railway buff from childhood, trains were his life. *Railway Age* named him its Railroader of the Year in 1999. Michigan State University established a chair in rail management in his name. He was described on the cover of *Trains* magazine as a man who "defied adversity."

On the other hand, according to Railway Workers United, a North America-wide group of railway workers, "the modus operandi for all of Burkhardt's adventures in railroading is to fire as many employees as possible, grind down the wages of the ones who remain and maximize the profits for himself and his fellow investors." His friend and sometime business partner Henry Posner said Burkhardt's passionate temperament was his greatest strength, but also his greatest weakness. Unlike the owners of most major North American railways, Burkhardt was a practitioner with intimate knowledge of the business.

His first major railroad venture was Wisconsin Central. This was the line that CN would eventually buy. But back in 1987, it was owned by the other major Canadian player, CP. Burkhardt bought it from CP and ran it from 1987 to 1999.

Burkhardt pushed one cost-saving idea in particular that would be a harbinger of the Lac-Mégantic disaster. Crew sizes had been shrinking for a decade; Burkhardt pioneered the single-crew concept. But his first effort, at Wisconsin Central, was opposed by its union and blocked by the state government. State congressman John Dobyns said: "Burkhardt doesn't care about public safety. He thinks only of profits."

An incident in 1996 gave credence to that statement. A Wisconsin

Central train carrying liquefied petroleum gas and propane derailed and exploded in Weyauwega, Wisconsin, forcing the evacuation of three thousand people — luckily, without the loss of life — and causing $20 million US in damage. An investigation by the National Transportation Safety Board blamed the crash on shoddy maintenance, caused in turn by inadequate employee training. Burkhardt denied this was the cause.

After losing a battle to buy out his partners, Burkhardt was forced off Wisconsin Central's board of directors by partners angry at the impact his direction was having on share prices. He sold his interest to CN in 2001 and went on to create Rail World, Inc., a private holding company based in Rosemont, a suburb of Chicago. Burkhardt was the controlling shareholder. Billing itself as a company specializing in "privatizations and restructurings," Rail World would house a growing stable of railway assets in the US and abroad.

"Fast Eddie" managed the privatization and restructuring of railways in the United Kingdom, New Zealand, Poland and Estonia. Posner called the last of these "a pipeline on wheels," created to transport oil from Russia to the Baltic Sea. It was a precursor to the North American oil-by-rail boom and a demonstration to Burkhardt of a lucrative specialty.

Burkhardt formed the corporate entity Montreal, Maine and Atlantic Railway in 2002, and in January 2003, acquired the assets of three bankrupt railways in Quebec, Maine and Vermont. Montreal, Maine and Atlantic Railway was a regional carrier with 825 kilometres of track, including a section formerly owned by CP running from Montreal through Lac-Mégantic to Maine.

As controlling shareholder, with 73 per cent of Montreal, Maine and Atlantic Railway's equity, Burkhardt appointed himself chair of the railway's board and installed Robert Grindrod as president and CEO. The railway's head office was in Hermon, Maine, a suburb of Bangor. The headquarters of its Canadian subsidiary was a dilapidated train station in Farnham, Quebec — but it was incorporated in Nova Scotia, thanks to the province's preferential tax rate. Montreal, Maine and Atlantic Railway Canada was at the bottom of the corporate ownership ladder, three rungs (Montreal, Maine and Atlantic Railway Canada, Montreal, Maine and Atlantic Railway, Rail World, Inc.) removed from Burkhardt's holding company at the top.

Burkhardt had on the surface an unlikely partner in Montreal, Maine and Atlantic Railway: the province of Quebec, in the form of the Caisse de depôts et placement du Québec, the pension fund of the province's public employees. The fund's investment mandate included the integration of environmental, social and governance criteria. In the years ahead, these considerations were subordinated, given the need to prop up a rail line that was economically vital to the Eastern Townships region. The fund injected $7 million in equity and a loan of $7.7 million. As the second-largest equity partner, the fund had a seat on the railway's board.[1]

Montreal, Maine and Atlantic Railway immediately cut employee wages by 40 per cent and, as the forestry industry extended its slump, the company continued to lay off staff and to reduce expenditures on track and equipment maintenance. By 2010, its workforce had shrunk to half of what it was in 2006.

Where Burkhardt had failed to introduce one-man crews in Wisconsin, in Maine he succeeded, with the acquiescence of the Federal Railroad Administration. The difference was that Maine's primary industries were dependent on the railway, giving Burkhardt leverage he did not enjoy in more economically diversified Wisconsin.[2]

Burkhardt insisted that single-person trains actually improved safety because members of the crew couldn't distract each other. Jerrod Briggs, an engineer who quit rather than submit to this idea, told the *Toronto Star*: "If you have two people watching, you can catch a mistake. It was all about cutting, cutting, cutting. It's just an example of putting company profits ahead of public safety."[3]

A few years later, Burkhardt introduced a radio-controlled system that allowed an operator equipped with a belt pack to remotely move trains around a yard. He calculated the cost of equipping one locomotive with the system was about the same as the annual salary and benefits of one worker.

Despite Burkhardt's cost-cutting, the railway continued to struggle financially.

REGULATORS CEDE POWER OVER SAFETY TO COMPANIES

In 2001, the Liberal government introduced a safety management system model of railway safety regulation. While the name sounded good, it spelled a further retreat from direct oversight, granting companies more discretion in balancing costs and safety.

Safety management systems are developed and managed by the rail companies themselves, according to regulatory criteria established by Transport Canada. Plans are overseen and audited by Transport Canada safety personnel. At least that was the theory. The ongoing clawback of Transport Canada's resources and powers under the Liberals left it ill-equipped to oversee this system of voluntary compliance.

The safety management system regime claimed to be a more effective way to reduce accidents, since it required companies to demonstrate that they were taking the lead in managing risks and inculcating a safety culture within their organizations. The approach was seen as a win-win: good for business, less costly for government at a time of fiscal retrenchment and a way to improve safety. Moreover, delegating responsibility for risk management to companies provided government with a cover in the event of regulatory failure.

Yet the adoption of safety management systems was a major surrender of Transport Canada's direct-oversight authority. While Transport Canada spokespeople insisted that safety management systems would constitute an additional layer to conventional regulation, no additional oversight resources were actually provided. On the contrary, resources continued to be squeezed, and the number of unannounced on-site inspections dwindled, replaced by document review by poorly trained inspectors-turned-auditors: a paper exercise. Euphemistically referred to as co-regulation, safety management systems were in effect industry self-regulation.

The new regime was introduced around the same time that American hedge funds and private equity funds, as well as railroad hardliners like Harrison and Burkhardt, were taking control of a now fully privatized Canadian freight railway system. Their confrontational style toward both the regulator and workers was not conducive to meeting safety management system goals. Indeed, the advent of safety management systems coincided with Burkhardt's entry onto the Canadian scene. Montreal, Maine and Atlantic Railway duly submitted a safety management system plan to Transport Canada, where it sat in a drawer, invisible to railway employees and ignored by Transport Canada.

Early on in the life of Montreal, Maine and Atlantic Railway, Burkhardt tried to get permission to run his trains in Canada with single-person crews. He could point to a precedent: the Quebec North Shore and Labrador Railway. Owned by Iron Ore Company of Canada, the firm where Mulroney had been CEO, the line transported ore from mines at Wabush, Newfoundland, to the port of Sept-Îles, Quebec.

Shortly after the line began this practice in 1996, one of its trains crashed into a parked train. A Transportation Safety Board investigation determined that single-person operations were one of the causes of the accident. After lengthy negotiations among the company, Transport Canada and the union, sixty-nine rigorous safety conditions were imposed that the railway would have to meet to resume the practice. So when Burkhardt applied for the same leeway, Transport Canada advised that he too would have to meet these conditions. Burkhardt thought the bar had been set too high and, discouraged, put the idea aside.

Montreal, Maine and Atlantic Railway had conflict-ridden labour-management relations. The inclination of the intermediate and senior management was to punish any behaviour that was not expressly ordered.[4] On the other hand, they tolerated deviation from safety rules governing issues such as train securement, especially when costs were involved.

By the same token, employees were discouraged from taking initiatives to enhance safety. Although Montreal, Maine and Atlantic Railway had a whistleblower provision in its Safety Management Plan, it was never used. Employees believed that using the provision would result not in remediation but recrimination.

It was a culture that fostered disengagement and led most employees to focus on protecting their own hides from blame rather than exposing situations of potential danger.[5] Employees who complained were invited to go work at McDonald's. A former insider characterized relations as the "normalization of deviance."

GOODBYE TO THE PRECAUTIONARY PRINCIPLE

Concurrent with developments in the railway sector, the Liberal government was advancing a broader deregulation agenda under the rubric of "smart regulation." As with the safety management system regime, it was framed as providing all things to all people: protecting health, safety and the environment, promoting growth and innovation and reducing the burden on corporations. The inference of the term "smart regulation" was that the previous approach of government-controlled regulation was *not* smart. In fact, it was a stand-in for direct regulation in an environment of fiscal austerity and continued government withdrawal from the economy.

The driving force behind the smart-regulation initiative was the Canadian Council of Chief Executives. Meanwhile, smart regulation was championed internally within the Privy Council and across departments, and strongly endorsed by the Liberal government.

The Privy Council struck the External Advisory Committee on Smart Regulation to flesh out the policy. The recommendations of this business-dominated panel became the 2005 Smart Regulation Action Plan, which in turn became the basis for the Liberal government's regulatory policy.[6]

A key element of the new regulatory policy was its definition of risk assessment. A 2001 Royal Society of Canada expert panel had asserted the primacy of the precautionary principle in protecting the public interest: err on the side of caution, identify potential risks, don't deploy until risk uncertainties are greatly reduced and place the primary burden of proof on companies to demonstrate that their products and activities do not pose unacceptable risks.[7] The smart regulation approach stood the precautionary principle on its head, holding that there was no need to act until harm had been proven by the regulator.

The deregulation train gained more momentum in 2005, when Prime Minister Paul Martin, along with his Mexican and American counterparts, launched the Security and Prosperity Partnership initiative. Aimed at easing the border logjams created in the name of security by the US following the 9/11 attacks, the partnership also sought to dismantle "unnecessary" regulations, to establish a forum for harmonizing differences and to ease the mobility of capital, goods, services and management personnel.

But the train hadn't finished accelerating. In the 2006 election, Martin was defeated by the Conservative party and Stephen Harper, a neoliberal so hard-line that he would overshadow his predecessors.

CHAPTER 3

Oil-Lobby Power, Railway-Lobby Power

The signal event in Alberta's history — and a turning point for Canada — was the discovery of oil near Leduc in the late 1950s.

Oil shifted the province's economic and political axis. Where Albertan politics had always been defined by agriculture and religion, the election of Progressive Conservatives led by Peter Lougheed in 1971 brought oil front and centre.

Lougheed saw oil as a vehicle to advance the province's social and economic well-being. His government created publicly owned enterprises in the sector, levied taxes and royalties to retain a significant share of oil wealth in government coffers and pioneered the creation of a sovereign wealth fund — the Alberta Heritage Savings Trust Fund — to put some of the oil windfall away for a rainy day. All these measures sought to stave off the "resource curse" that has hamstrung many petroleum-rich countries.

However, Lougheed's successors, especially Premier Ralph Klein, reversed these efforts. By the time Harper came to power in 2006, Alberta had largely succumbed to the "petro-state" malaise. The petroleum industry had captured the policy-making apparatus. Alberta had become an "oil deep state," in the words of former provincial Liberal leader Kevin Taft.[1]

In a petro-state, petroleum enjoys a dominant role in the economy, and governments are highly dependent on revenue from the industry. In Canada, the shift in power changed everything from the national identity to the fate of communities that, like Lac-Mégantic, would be drawn into the new national narrative, with no say in the matter.

However, a country's pre-existing institutional landscape determines how deeply petro-wealth can influence public institutions: political parties, elections, laws, policies, regulations, the civil service, the courts, the media and academic institutions.[2]

Norway is the exception to the resource curse rule. Prior to the discovery of oil, Norway — whose economy is roughly the same size as Alberta's and which experienced its oil rush at about the same time — was a modern state with strong public-sector institutions, a robust and progressive tax system, a highly educated population with deeply rooted egalitarian values and a cross-party consensus on how to manage petro-wealth. These characteristics enabled Norway to "sow" petroleum into a huge financial asset belonging to the country's citizens. Norway's sovereign wealth fund now exceeds $1 trillion US, whereas the Alberta fund has a mere $13 billion US. Most Norwegians are well off as a consequence, while Albertans have negligible collective savings to show for decades of petroleum wealth extraction.

Harper was a product of the emerging Alberta petro-state. His father worked as an accountant for Imperial Oil, the Canadian subsidiary of Exxon. After growing up in Toronto, Harper moved to Calgary, studied economics at the University of Calgary and worked summers for Esso, the retail arm of Imperial Oil.

First elected to Parliament in 1993 as part of the Reform Party wave, Harper quit after one term to head a right-wing libertarian advocacy group, the National Citizens Coalition. During his time out of office, Harper developed close ties with influential conservatives in the US, including the Koch brothers.

The Kochs owned a giant, privately held petroleum corporation with vast investments in the Alberta oil sands, valued in the tens of billions of dollars and estimated to cover some 4,500 square kilometres of boreal forest. The largest exporters of Alberta bitumen, the Kochs are known for their political donations to right-wing causes, including Canadian climate change skeptics like the Fraser Institute — the favourite think tank of Harper himself.

Harper returned to Parliament in 2002 as leader of the Canadian Alliance, the reinvented Reform Party. Though Harper never revealed his leadership bid's major donors, his campaign was financed largely by petroleum companies, according to former American Vice President Al Gore.

As the next step in his quest to become prime minister, Harper orchestrated the merger of the Alliance with the moribund Progressive Conservative party to form the rebranded Conservative Party of Canada in 2003, with himself installed as leader of the now official opposition.

When he completed the final step to power in the 2006 federal election, Harper was on record as hating taxes and regulation. The previous generation of deregulation, privatization and trade initiatives provided a solid foundation to build on.

Harper was preoccupied with the idea that Alberta should replace central Canada as the primary engine of the Canadian economy. Shortly after becoming prime minister, he spoke to a group of international investors in London, England, urging them to recognize "Canada's emergence as a global energy powerhouse — the emerging energy superpower our government intends to build." Harper could point to the recent confirmation by the US Department of Energy that Canada's unconventional oil fields — the Alberta bitumen or tar sands — contained the world's third-largest reserves of recoverable oil, after Saudi Arabia and Venezuela.

Investors responded enthusiastically to Harper's invitation, setting off an unprecedented bitumen boom. Foreign direct investment grew rapidly. Although the US still accounted for the majority of foreign ownership in the Alberta oil patch, European and Asian investors were increasing their overall share.

The riddle of how to separate the oil from the sand it was found in had been solved years earlier by treating bitumen deposits with hot water to separate out sand and clay. An extended period of $100-per-barrel oil made the venture highly profitable. Bitumen was scraped out from huge open pits or extracted from in situ operations buried deep under the boreal muskeg. While a portion was then upgraded to synthetic oil, some 60 per cent of bitumen was combined with volatile petrochemicals called diluents — which make the crude flow better —then shipped out to refineries and ports across the continent.

Bitumen production grew rapidly, reaching 1.8 million barrels per day by 2012. Crude oil prices, which had jumped from $20 per barrel in 2002 to a peak of $134 per barrel in June 2008, plunged briefly in the wake of the 2008–09 global economic crisis. But by 2011 they had climbed back to $99 per barrel. As oil production, exports and investment grew, so too did the Canadian dollar appreciate, reaching parity with the US dollar. Confirming its status as a petro-currency, the high dollar hindered exports of manufactured goods from Canada's industrial heartland in Ontario and Quebec.[3]

As prime minister, Harper brought an Alberta petro-state style of governance to the federal government. Distrustful of the Ottawa bureaucracy, public-sector unions and the media establishment, he clamped down on independent-minded ministers, snuffed out public servants' communications with the media and muzzled scientists from speaking publicly about their research. He appointed deputy ministers and other senior agency officials he knew would toe the line without question, and got rid of those who did not. *The Economist* described him as a "political predator" with little regard for science, due process or the media.[4]

Harper exerted tight political control to ensure oil company priorities were being carried out. The revolving-door syndrome accelerated as personnel moved between the oil industry and federal departments, agencies, boards and commissions. Senior Prime Minister's Office staffers transferred easily to oil-lobby firms on Parliament Hill. In his book *Oil's Deep State*, Taft provides a striking example of how the petroleum industry inserted itself into federal energy policy and regulatory infrastructure. The tools were two oil industry–created organizations that worked behind the scenes with top federal civil servants and their provincial counterparts, as well as with major universities, to shape policies and regulations consistent with petroleum-industry priorities.[5]

The Energy Policy Institute of Canada was a not-for-profit organization comprised of Canada's largest petroleum corporations, with the sole purpose of advancing the industry's commercial interests. Its board included prominent members of Canada's business elite with close ties to both the Alberta and federal governments: David Emerson, a former cabinet minister in both Liberal and Conservative governments; Tom d'Aquino, the recently retired CEO of the Canadian Council of Chief Executives; and Frank McKenna, who had been premier of New Brunswick and ambassador to Washington, and who had strong ties to Irving Oil and Toronto-Dominion Bank.

Convicted fraudster, Bruce Carson, then an aide in the Harper Office, was a key player in shepherding this public-private policy partnership. While at the Prime Minister's Office, Carson was a founding co-chair of the Energy Policy Institute of Canada, from which he drew a hefty salary. He was at the same time executive director of the Canadian School of Energy and Environment at the University of Calgary, a position he used to ensure the academic community was working closely with the energy companies on policy reports that aligned with their commercial interests, while giving the appearance of scholarly independence.

Cassie Doyle, deputy minister of the Department of Natural Resources, worked closely with Carson. Kevin Lynch, the Harper-appointed clerk of the Privy Council — Canada's top civil servant — was brought on board to ensure government policies were fully aligned with industry priorities in a unified energy strategy focused on oil sands development. This behind-closed-doors collaboration between the industry and the highest levels of government bureaucracy represented an unprecedented rupture of the boundary that traditionally separated the two.

Besides creating these highly effective informal pathways to policy formation, the oil industry shaped policy through more conventional lobbying activities. A study by the Polaris Institute found that between July 2008 and November 2012, lobbyists acting on behalf of individual corporations or industry associations in the fossil-fuel sphere had more than 2,700 oral communications with politicians and senior departmental and agency officials. The most prominent lobby, the Canadian Association of Petroleum Producers, recorded 536 such communications. By contrast, the largest environmental umbrella group, the Climate Action Network, had six.

The oil lobby saw the fruits of its labours in the actions of the Harper government. Recommendations for relaxing regulatory and statutory requirements for pipeline and oil sands project approvals were adopted virtually unchanged. Many of these changes were enacted through massive omnibus budget bills, and thus were never properly debated in Parliament or scrutinized by parliamentary committees.

On a neighbouring front, changes to the *Canadian Environmental Assessment Act* eliminated 90 per cent of federal environmental reviews of major industrial projects, such as pipelines. For the remaining assessments, it transferred responsibility to the industry-friendly National Energy Board, which was now under cabinet control. Former BC Hydro chairman Marc Eliesen withdrew from hearings considering the Kinder Morgan pipeline proposal, claiming the board had been captured by the oil and gas industry. In an investigative series for the *National Observer*, Mike De Souza found instances of the board agreeing to whitewash audits of Enbridge and TransCanada pipeline spills.

No stone was left unturned. The Harper government shut down government-funded organizations conducting research and analysis on climate change and other environmental issues. It also launched major lobbying and advertising campaigns to advance oil industry interests. It successfully lobbied European governments to prevent a European Union ban on imports of bitumen based on its classification as a dirty fuel. Cabinet members, led by Natural Resources Minister Joe Oliver, railed against environmental and other non-governmental organizations, which threatened, in his words, "to hijack our regulatory system to achieve their radical ideological agenda." Ottawa drew up an enemies list, which it used to attack charities with a series of audits designed to silence their policy work. (The organization I headed, the Canadian Centre for Policy Alternatives, was among those targeted.) As noted above, the Harper regime muzzled federal government scientists, preventing them from sharing their research on the impacts of fossil fuels on climate change. And it took the unprecedented measure of withdrawing Canada from its treaty commitments under the Kyoto Protocol.

SAFETY OVERSIGHT DETERIORATES

The oil companies and railways were closely allied. Railways were the largest transporters of coal, the original fossil fuel. CP, now headquartered in Calgary, was an integral part of the oil patch culture.

As bitumen production was ramping up, the shrinking pipeline capacity and looming roadblocks to new pipeline construction were evident to both industries. Railways saw the potential of this lucrative new cargo. Both saw rail as an alternative to ease pipeline transportation bottlenecks and also saw the value of rail-pipeline complementary networks to reach a diversity of markets and overcome price disadvantages to which Alberta, as a landlocked producer, was vulnerable. Aligned with Harper government ambitions, the rail and petroleum lobbies were a seamless web of power and influence in pursuit of a common goal.

On the regulatory side, the railways were already in the driver's seat. According to a former government insider, "The railways, through the Railway Association of Canada, got everything they asked for . . . it was rubber-stamped. It got worse and worse under Harper."

There was, however, dissent. The Canadian Rail Operating Rules, a component of the 1988 *Railway Safety Act*, were often criticized by the Transportation Safety Board, unions and independent experts as being too vague and inadequately enforced. Companies were given too much latitude and granted too many exemptions, according to railway unions.

The process for granting these exemptions was opaque. Brian Stevens, rail director for the Unifor union, testified before the House of Commons transport committee: "We have a regulatory regime and then there's a back door [for railways] to walk themselves out of the rules." The union representing Transport Canada's railway inspectors, the Union of Canadian Transportation Employees, stated in a brief to the Commons transport committee: "[I]t is often difficult for individual rail safety inspectors to understand why a company receives an exemption in specific circumstances."[6]

The Transportation Safety Board could make recommendations to Transport Canada but had no power to compel action. And Transport Canada routinely dragged its feet on their implementation. One aspect of the Canadian Rail Operating Rules that was particularly vague with implications for Lac-Mégantic concerned train securement rules.[7] They required only the application of "sufficient handbrakes" to hold a train, leaving companies wide discretion to make their own decisions about securement and associated safety defences. The Transportation Safety Board criticized the rules for being performance-based rather than prescriptive.[8] Transport Canada also allowed the practice of leaving trains unlocked and unattended on a main track, another factor at Lac-Mégantic. It rejected a Transportation Safety Board recommendation to lock unattended locomotives as "unwarranted."[9]

Transport Canada also failed to act on Transportation Safety Board warnings dating back to the early 1990s that the standard DOT-111 tank cars were not safe for transporting dangerous goods. Yet again, this would be a factor in Lac-Mégantic. The board's warning was based on no less than twenty-five accident investigations since 1991. However, the petroleum and chemical industries — which owned the vast majority of tank cars — were not willing to invest in stronger, more crash-resistant tank cars. And railways, which had no investments of their own at stake, were less than aggressive in their demands for upgrades.

The Canadian Rail Operating Rules were amended or added to in the years that followed, mostly by the industry, sometimes on the advice of Transport Canada. Transport Canada had to approve rule changes, though it was largely a rubber stamp.

The most comprehensive changes occurred in 2008. Not just Montreal, Maine and Atlantic Railway but the industry as a whole had been frustrated for years that single-person train operations faced a high regulatory hurdle after it was identified as a cause of the 1996 Quebec North Shore and Labrador accident discussed in Chapter 2.

But here too relief came by way of the industry's drafting of major amendments to the Canadian Rail Operating Rules. They created a loophole, General Rule M, that eliminated virtually every previous rule that had required two or more persons to act in a given situation.[10] It removed the unions' right to negotiate crew size during collective bargaining, as well as rules requiring companies to establish supplementary safety devices such as electronically based collision warning systems.

Senior Transport Canada officials were highly supportive of the new, industry-friendly approach. According to one former insider, their approach was: "'Let's get it done, let's make it happen'; not 'What are the safety risks?'" John Baird was appointed transport minister in October 2008, just in time to approve the railways' rewrite of the operating rules. Transport Canada did not conduct — or require the industry to conduct — a risk assessment to ensure that one-person crews offered an equivalent level of safety to that offered by two-person crews. Transport Canada did, however, commission a study by the National Research Council to get a better understanding of the issue. With the Canadian Rail Operating Rules in place, the introduction of the safety management system regulatory regime in 2001, described in Chapter 2, represented a quantum leap in the ability of railways to regulate themselves. But major flaws in the regime soon came to light.

A 2006 internal Transport Canada audit found "incomplete" and "inconsistent" reports from inspections related to dangerous goods, and estimated that levels of non-compliance were very high. The then chief of marine transportation security and regulatory affairs, Ian Bron, submitted a report to the deputy minister in December 2006 expressing concern that Transport Canada was "implementing a system of regulation that was effectively a rubber-stamp checklist. Paperwork was being examined, but no inspectors were on the ground doing proper tests of the systems to make sure they worked."[11]

Bron was hounded for years for speaking up. Yet he had other experts on his side. A report the following year by the Canada Safety Council described the safety management system regime as an accident waiting to happen: "[It] allows rail companies to regulate themselves, removing the federal government's ability to protect Canadians and their environment, and allowing the industry to hide critical safety information from the public." It urged the government to restore Transport Canada's direct oversight role.[12]

A 2007 government-commissioned *Railway Safety Act* Review Panel, while not proposing to change the safety management system regime in principle, cautioned that it required a major shift in thinking by both the regulator and the railways.[13] Its report found "Transport Canada . . . was not provided with sufficient human and financial resources, and the appropriate skill sets . . . to effectively manage and oversee Safety Management Systems."

Overall, the panel concluded that "Transport Canada is inadequately resourced to carry out its many responsibilities in the area of railway safety." This was not the kind of input the austerity-minded Harper government was inclined to heed. Nor did Transport Canada act on its advice to monitor more closely short-line railways like Montreal, Maine and Atlantic Railway.

In a 2007 *Transportation Law Journal* article, lawyer Wayne Benedict, a one-time locomotive engineer, urged the government to restore rail safety regulatory power to Transport Canada.[14] "Allowing companies to manage their own safety," he wrote, "is not adequately protecting the interests of the Canadian public, the Canadian environment or the Canadian railway workers. To private railway companies, whose *raison d'être* is to make maximum profits, expensive investments in safety . . . will always be subordinate to other competitive factors when subjected to cost-benefit analysis."[15] Benedict ended his article by invoking the memory of some major train derailments: "What the future holds for Canada's railway safety regulatory system is difficult to discern. However, if the trend . . . continues unchecked it is only a matter of time before Canadians are confronted with another Mississauga, Hinton, Edson or worse."[16]

Several Transportation Safety Board investigations also found deficiencies in the implementation of safety management systems, such as not conducting risk assessments for significant changes in operations. The board added safety management systems to its 2010 watchlist, whose purpose is to alert industry, Transport Canada and the public to outstanding safety issues: "Railways (and other modes) are not always identifying and mitigating risks through their Safety Management Systems, and Transport Canada audits are not always effective."

All told, the safety net in the rail freight industry was frayed and vulnerable, existing more on paper than in the real world. And the system was starting to be tested by a boom in a commodity that was explosive — in the political sense and, more importantly, in a literal sense.

CHAPTER 4

Pipeline on Wheels

Most of Canada was in the grip of recession in 2008–09, but the Alberta bitumen boom churned on with only a minor hiccup. Meanwhile, in North Dakota, another revolution in unconventional oil was under way: the Bakken boom. Technological innovations — horizontal drilling and hydraulic fracturing — were freeing up vast deposits of oil trapped in shale formations, with spectacular results.

Fracking of oil and gas entails a host of environmental dangers, sufficient to inspire a prohibition of the practice in jurisdictions such as Quebec and New Brunswick. But to North Dakota, fracking was the manna that took the state from backwater to prosperity. By 2012, it was the second-largest oil-producing state, after Texas.

The Klondike-style black-gold rush created tens of thousands of jobs. The boom had something in common with the new attitude in the rail freight industry: safety was not top of mind. Reportedly, one worker died every six weeks.

North Dakota was ill-equipped for the boom, in housing — towns suddenly tripled in size — and, critically, infrastructure. Absent were refineries and a well-developed pipeline system. Moreover, Bakken oil had to compete for what pipeline space existed with increasing volumes of bitumen flowing south from Alberta.

How to get product to market? Rail seemed an obvious solution. A network of tracks already existed in the state. The system, it was true, needed major refurbishment. Rail lines had been largely abandoned. Much of the track and bridge infrastructure would need major upgrades.

Another challenge was loading the oil efficiently. The problem was cracked by EOG Resources, a surviving offshoot of the disgraced Enron Corporation. EOG invented a technique that could fill an uninterrupted chain of one hundred tank cars, each carrying more than seven hundred barrels of crude oil, in half a day.[1]

In 2008, EOG built its first loading terminal. Thus was born the pipeline on wheels. Others soon followed EOG's example. The terminals were quickly green-lit. And regulators in both the US and Canada did not distinguish between a train with one car and one with a hundred cars.

Pipeline, rail and trucking companies were investing huge sums in infrastructure to get product to market. Canadian-owned Enbridge, one of the largest pipeline companies in North America, invested $1.2 billion US in North Dakota in 2012, not only to expand its pipeline infrastructure but also to construct rail-loading facilities — a rail hub in the town of Berthold — to connect to the national network of Burlington Northern Santa Fe. Enbridge also built a truck-to-rail facility and a hub connecting small pipelines to the rail system.

Rail enabled both Bakken producers and Alberta bitumen producers to circumvent comparatively low prices they were getting due to pipeline bottlenecks, which, in an oversupplied market, allowed buyers to bid down prices. And, absent pipelines to tidewater, there was no place else for Canadian to go: almost 80 per cent of Canadian oil production and virtually all exports went to the US.

And rail connected producers to coastal refineries, such as Irving's in New Brunswick, that did not have pipeline access, and that wanted a substitute for overseas imported crude that they were buying at the much more expensive world prices.

Bakken production had reached 770,000 barrels per day by 2012, with recoverable reserves estimated at forty-five billion barrels. Major oil companies — among them Western Petroleum, a subsidiary of World Fuels Services Corp., later implicated in the Lac-Mégantic tragedy — were at the forefront of the production windfall.

By 2012, more than 60 per cent of Bakken oil, some 450,000 barrels per day, was shipped out by rail from eighteen rail-loading sites throughout North Dakota. Burlington Northern Santa Fe, by far the largest transporter of Bakken crude, had increased its loading capacity to one million barrels (or around sixteen unit trains) per day. (A unit train is an uninterrupted chain of typically between 80 and 110 tank cars. It contains no cars containing non-volatile product placed intermittently to limit fire in the case of a derailment.)

Oil by rail in the US grew from 9,500 tank carloads in 2009 to 415,000 in 2013, the vast majority from North Dakota. Railway revenue from oil skyrocketed from $25.8 million US to $2.2 billion US during this period.

The number of reported oil train "incidents" skyrocketed too, rising from one to 144.

For the residents of faraway Lac-Mégantic, a fateful decision in the boom was taken by World Fuels to form a joint venture with Dakota Plains Holdings Inc., a local landowner, to rebuild an old rail line near New Town, North Dakota. Here it created the Dakota Plains terminal, which sourced oil from local producers.

The Dakota Plains terminal joined three others in the region serviced by CP — the second-largest transporter of Bakken oil and the only other company besides Burlington Northern Santa Fe that owned track in North Dakota. CP's position was strengthened by also being a major transporter of sand, an essential ingredient in the fracking process. As Bakken boomed, so too did CP.

POP CANS ON WHEELS

There were a number of inconvenient facts that the oil and railway industries ignored in their rush to export Bakken crude. Firstly, they were using tank cars deemed unsafe for such dangerous goods.

The standard US Department of Transport DOT-111 (also called TC-111 in Canada) was considered the Ford Pinto of tank cars: a "pop can on wheels," according Eric de Place, a researcher at the Seattle-based Sightline Institute. It was designed for carrying products like corn oil. It had a thin shell and no head shields at either end to prevent puncturing in the event of a derailment. Both Canadian and US transportation safety boards had warned since the 1990s that these railcars were unsafe for carrying dangerous goods. But the warnings went unheeded by regulators under pressure from the oil and railway industries. By 2013, almost half of the North American standard DOT-111 tank car fleet was being used to transport flammable liquids.

The other inconvenient fact was that Bakken crude had disturbing qualities. As early as 2010, studies found that the chemicals used to extract shale oil made it unusually volatile and toxic. And there was evidence that chemicals used in the fracking process were damaging tank car interiors. A team of North Dakota government geologists noticed increasing concentrations of hydrogen sulphide in the oil — a health and environmental hazard, and a corrosive compound. The team proposed further research but did not follow through, and there was no examination of the interaction between Bakken oil and injected fracking fluids. One of the team members told *Globe and Mail* journalist Grant Robertson that one of the reasons for not continuing their research was that "we didn't get a whole lot of co-operation from the industry."

A 2011–12 inspection of North Dakota loading facilities by the Pipeline and Hazardous Materials Safety Administration found that tank cars were being overloaded, and that suitable cars were in short supply. Compliance was difficult to enforce because there were so many companies involved. The resulting report, *North Dakota: The Next Hazardous Materials Frontier*, found that shippers were regularly overloading tank cars, which at times were "out of specification."[2] Some companies were mislabelling the oil as less flammable than it actually was. "The pressure to ship those cars was more than the risk of failure in transit or discovery by Federal Railroad Administration." The report advised truck drivers and inspectors to take special precautions: "Fire-retardant clothing, and grounded equipment, truck and railcars are mandatory due to the high flammability of the crude and possibility of static discharge."

The Pipeline and Hazardous Materials Safety Administration and the Federal Railroad Administration are agencies within the US Department of Transportation. The former agency's primary mandate is setting and enforcing regulations regarding hazardous materials. The latter promulgates and enforces rail safety regulations more generally.

Although the Pipeline and Hazardous Materials Safety Administration was aware of the dangers, it did not require companies to remove the explosive gases from Bakken crude or the injected fluids, such as naphtha. It focused instead on the tank cars, caving in to the argument of the American Petroleum Institute, the industry's foremost trade association, that Bakken crude was no more volatile than conventional crude oil. The issue of the dangerous contents was shunted off to the Department of Energy for further study.[3]

By 2012, the National Transportation Safety Board had concerns about the growing number of unit oil train shipments and the possibility of a major accident: "The risks are greater because of high concentrations of hazardous materials. Existing standards and regulations are insufficient." They were also concerned that in a Wild West environment, oversight was weak or non-existent. Echoing the concerns of the Pipeline and Hazardous Materials Safety Administration, the board reported that oil was routinely misclassified, tank cars were being overloaded, cars were in short supply and major gaps in safety regulation existed.

The North Dakota Industrial Commission, the division of the North Dakota Department of Mineral Resources that regulates oil and gas production, was scant help in addressing these concerns. A rubber stamp for the oil industry, it allowed workers to be exposed to radioactive material brought to the surface in fracking; the material was discarded as if it were regular garbage. A wilful blindness ruled: The Department of Mineral Resources told the *Globe and Mail* it was not aware that Bakken oil was unusually volatile.

By October 2011, the Association of American Railroads had recommended design changes to improve the safety of DOT-111 tank cars.[4]

These modifications were incorporated into the new CPC-1232 model of car. Both American and Canadian transportation safety agencies recommended that flammable liquids be transported exclusively in the upgraded cars. However, neither regulator required existing tank cars to be retrofitted to the higher standard. Oil and tank-car leasing companies continued to resist calls for upgrades. By 2013, 80 per cent of the Canadian tanker fleet and two-thirds of the American fleet carrying crude oil were conventional DOT-111 tank cars.

In May 2012, Enbridge complained to the Federal Energy Regulatory Commission, the agency that regulates the transmission of oil and other energy products, about the dangerously high hydrogen sulphide levels in Bakken crude. In response, the commission allowed Enbridge to block crude oil with excessive sulphide vapours from entering its pipeline.

There was a better solution available. Oil fracked in Bakken's sister shale formation — Eagle Ford, in Texas — had its volatile components removed before it was loaded and processed in nearby refineries. But no such procedure was required prior to loading oil onto tank cars in the Bakken region, which had no refineries. The volatile components were removed only once they reached their destination.

ADVANTAGE: RAIL

If the dangers of transporting oil by rail were obvious to at least some observers, the advantages were even more clear-cut for the oil industry. Rail was more expensive, it was true. But that was offset by another dollar argument, the pipeline logjam.

Crucially, unlike with pipelines, for rail there was no need to gain regulatory permission. The tracks were already in place. By the same token, in both the US and Canada, rail-loading facilities did not have to clear the same environmental assessments and other regulatory tests that pipelines faced. What's more, they were rapidly constructed, cheaper than pipelines and produced a faster rate of return. Rail-loading capacity in Alberta and Saskatchewan grew by leaps and bounds.

CP, which had moved its headquarters from Montreal to Calgary in 1996 to be closer to its major freight — grain and fossil fuels — was now identified as a Western Canadian company. It had forged close rela-tionships with the petroleum industry, which dominated the economic landscape and shaped Alberta government policy. It was becoming an integral part of Canada's oil transportation strategy under the Harper Conservatives.

CN, meanwhile, had direct access to the east and west coasts, and to the Gulf of Mexico. It moved 30,000 carloads in 2012 and estimated that number would more than double the following year. CP's network, supplemented by interchange agreements with other railways, greatly expanded its reach as well. Bitumen was transported — usually in the diluted form ("dilbit") — from the wellhead via feeder pipelines to two hubs in Alberta, which connected directly to both CN and CP rail net-works throughout North America. CN also had a direct rail line from the oil sands. For both railways, the unconventional oil bonanza was a lucrative new revenue stream.

Canada's oil-by-rail boom grew in lockstep with the American trend. Total shipments increased exponentially, from 500 tank carloads in 2009 to 160,000 by 2013. The number of oil train "incidents" rose from eight in 2011, the first year they were recorded by the Transportation Safety Board, to fifty-six in 2013. The ingredients for disaster were coming into view.

CHAPTER 5

A Crew of One

In 2009, with General Rule M in place, Montreal, Maine and Atlantic Railway got Transport Canada's permission for one-man American crews to drive trains across the border through largely uninhabited territory, to and from Nantes and nearby locations. When Montreal, Maine and Atlantic Railway pressed to be allowed to extend operating single-person crew trains through Quebec's Eastern Townships communities in 2011, Kevin Mosher was concerned. For he'd seen, close up, the company's attitude to safety.

Mosher, who had logged many years at CP, was the supervisor of one of Iron Road Railways' lines at the Farnham station when the company went bankrupt. Burkhardt bought the railway and renamed it Montreal, Maine and Atlantic Railway in 2003. In the resulting reorganization, Mosher, a qualified locomotive engineer, lost his supervisory position and returned to the union ranks.

In 2008, he was elected co-chair of Montreal, Maine and Atlantic Railway's labour-management health and safety committee. Although it was mandated under the *Canada Labour Code*, railway management never took the committee seriously. They rarely held the prescribed minimum annual number of meetings, provided no resources to the committee and at times excluded labour members from participating in "joint" workplace inspections. It fell to Mosher to compile minutes of meetings, record company responses to concerns and prepare reports to government. Occasionally, he would be asked to erase past records of company commitments that had not been met. He refused.

When Montreal, Maine and Atlantic Railway signalled it planned to go ahead with single-person crews from Farnham to Lac-Mégantic, Mosher did not reject the idea out of hand but wanted to ensure the change could be made safely. He contacted Quebec North Shore and Labrador, the only railway in Canada operating with single-person crews, to find out what measures it had in place to ensure safety. He then brought the results of his inquiries to the committee, requesting that the company consider them. But the other railway's safety practices were rejected and instead Montreal, Maine and Atlantic Railway drafted a letter to Transport Canada, which stated that both the company and its health and safety committee had agreed to proceed with single-person operations. It was, in Mosher's words, "a bunch of lies." They wanted Mosher to sign the letter; again, he refused.

Mosher then wrote to management, reiterating the changes he wanted to see adopted before Montreal, Maine and Atlantic Railway proceeded with single-person crews. He requested that the letter be forwarded to Transport Canada. Management not only refused, Mosher remembers: "They began to make my life hell." Frustrated at the unwillingness of the company to resolve a whole array of health and safety issues, he stepped down from the committee in May 2012. He knew it was time to leave Montreal, Maine and Atlantic Railway.

Mosher's story confirmed other accounts of "the normalization of deviance," observed by others at Montreal, Maine and Atlantic Railway. He described a lack of training and supervision, and a lack too of maintenance of the track and right-of-way. Locomotives often came back from the repair shop not repaired.

Mosher confirmed the later finding of the Sûreté du Québec, the provincial police, that most Montreal, Maine and Atlantic Railway employees did not know how to correctly secure their trains, as outlined in Rule 112 of the Canadian Rail Operating Rules.

Indeed, management even encouraged unsafe work practices. When engineers ran trains over the speed limit, supervisors approved, since it meant trains were arriving faster. Those employees who, like Mosher, followed the rules were harassed for logging longer travel times, which could spell additional costs: Once employees had hit a twelve-hour work limit, they had to be relieved.

According to Mosher, it took months and sometimes years for Montreal, Maine and Atlantic Railway to address issues raised by the health and safety committee. The effect, he said, was to foster a sense of resignation among staff at all levels. "Even the local supervisory staff were so tired of it all that nobody cared anymore and they were just there to collect their paycheque. Transport Canada would visit and find nonconformities that were never addressed, some even getting worse as time went on."

In the summer of 2012, Mosher applied for a job at the Arnaud Railway in Sept-Îles, Quebec. He was invited for an interview. He was granted a two-day leave and made flight arrangements for the trip. The day before his departure, his bosses, Quebec operations director Jean Demaître and his assistant, Michael Horan, revoked the leave. Mosher went anyway and learned on his return that he had been suspended.

But at least Mosher never had to drive oil trains by himself. He was offered the job at Arnaud, which he took up in September.

THE BIG PUSH FOR SOLO TRAINS

After successfully implementing stage one of the plan in 2010, Montreal, Maine and Atlantic Railway CEO Robert Grindrod signalled to Transport Canada officials in December 2011 that the railway intended to extend its single-person crew operation through eleven communities, including Farnham, Magog, Sherbrooke, Nantes and Lac-Mégantic. Grindrod said the railway had met with the mayors of the towns along the route and no concerns had been raised over the prospect of one-person crews.

However, United Steelworkers representative Richard Boudreault would later testify before the House of Commons transport committee that the implementation of one-person crews was made "without any consultation with the communities or with the unions." In an interview with the Radio-Canada investigative program *Enquête*, the mayor of Farnham, Josef Hüsler, also denied that any such meeting was held.

Also in December, Grindrod wrote to the Railway Association's director of regulatory policy, Kevin McKinnon, expressing his frustration with the pushback from the Quebec regional office of Transport Canada, located in Montreal, against extending single-person train operations: "The Montreal office has been against this from the start, and has been overruled by . . . Carlson from the start, thus I am having trouble understanding their attitude. Your help will be very much appreciated." ("Carlson" is senior Transport Canada bureaucrat Walter Carlson, about whom more below.)

McKinnon responded: "Leave this with me, Robert. I will make some calls."

Transport Canada had informed Montreal, Maine and Atlantic Railway that single-person train operation required a risk assessment. The railway produced an assessment in early 2012, but it contained major deficiencies. It did not address the risks of a lone operator performing tasks previously performed with a second crew member, such as securing a train at the end of the shift. It did not consider whether persons working alone could be subject to fatigue and cognitive degradation over the course of a shift. Nor did it put forward compensating measures to mitigate these risks.

Senior Transport Canada officials at headquarters did not think a new risk assessment was necessary. But the Montreal office again balked at Montreal, Maine and Atlantic Railway's request: "We consider that this major change in the operations exposes workers and surrounding communities to greater risks."

The sense of that view seems obvious — how can a train, especially one with many cars of dangerous cargo, be safely operated by a single person? And indeed an expert view backs up the common-sense one.

Former long-time railway employee and Transportation Board investigator Steve Callaghan — who had extensive experience with single-person trains on the Quebec North Shore and Labrador line — said that proceeding with solo trains without proper risk-mitigation measures was "insanity." Furthermore, according to Callaghan, the change could not be safely implemented without installing on-board fail-safe collision warning systems such as positive train control.

On February 3, 2012, in an email exchange with headquarters, Quebec Regional Director Luciano Martin wrote, "I would like [Montreal, Maine and Atlantic Railway] to explain how they will put the necessary rigour in their processes for extended single-person train operation when it is the application of the same basic processes that has led to past Transport Canada concerns and regulatory actions."

The railway had an appalling safety record. Documents obtained by *Enquête* revealed at least eight warnings were issued to the railway by Transport Canada between 2004 and 2012 regarding violations of train securement Rule 112. Inspectors found major defects in its safety management system, which went uncorrected. Its accident rate, according to the US Federal Railroad Administration, was three times the national average. Throughout 2011, inspectors with Transport Canada's Quebec office continued to document their concern about Montreal, Maine and Atlantic Railway's ability to operate safely. Nevertheless, Transport Canada failed to sanction the company.

Later that February, two months after the Railway Association of Canada executive promised to take care of Montreal, Maine and Atlantic Railway's problem, the railway and the Railway Association met with Transport Canada at its Quebec office in Montreal, whose staff remained adamantly opposed to solo trains and had refused to attend an earlier meeting between Carlson and Montreal, Maine and Atlantic Railway at the company's Maine head office. Another dissident was Daniel Lafontaine, chief of engineering, a Carlson subordinate in Ottawa.

Montreal, Maine and Atlantic Railway brought a strong contingent to the meeting: CEO Grindrod, general manager of transportation Lynne

Labonté and Jean Demaître, Montreal, Maine and Atlantic Railway's Quebec operations director. Burkhardt himself came up from Chicago to make sure resistance from the upstart Quebec office would not torpedo things.

At the meeting, Carlson advised the railway that it wasn't necessary for Transport Canada to approve the shift to single-person train operations, thanks to General Rule M (which, as related in Chapter 3, swept away virtually all rules mandating a second crew member). The only specific measure that Transport Canada would require was that the company place an oversized mirror on the side of the locomotive opposite from where the engineer sat.

It was a low-tech measure by any standard. Many countries permit single-person train operation, but in virtually all cases only where a remote-control, satellite-based protection system for monitoring and controlling train movements, such as positive train control, is in place. However such precautions are expensive, and thus contrary to Montreal, Maine and Atlantic Railway's motive for single-person train operation — to save money.

Some pushback followed the Transport Canada decision. The Union of Canadian Transport Employees, which represents Transport Canada inspectors, formally objected in a letter to Transport Minister Denis Lebel, citing Montreal, Maine and Atlantic Railway's poor safety record. The United Steelworkers, which represented Montreal, Maine and Atlantic Railway workers, also opposed the decision during contract negotiations, but was told by the federal mediator that the decision was outside the purview of collective bargaining.

WHERE THE BUCK STOPS

Who was responsible for the decision to permit this delinquent company to operate its massive oil trains with a single crewmember? Presumably, responsibility ultimately lies with Transport Minister Denis Lebel.

However, the Canadian Guidelines for Ministers written by Harper's Privy Council had been changed several years earlier. The 2007 guidelines explained ministerial responsibility as follows: "Ministers are individually responsible to Parliament and the prime minister for their own actions and those of their department, including the actions of all officials under their management and direction, whether or not the ministers had prior knowledge." However, by 2011 the guidelines had changed: "Ministerial accountability to Parliament does not mean that a minister is presumed to have knowledge of every matter that occurs within his or her department or portfolio, nor that the minister is necessarily required to accept blame for every matter."

The next question is: Where does the buck stop within Transport Canada? Recall from Chapter 1 that Transport Canada was a highly dysfunctional department. Communication within divisions was fragmented, information was not shared. A maze of boards, committees, blurred and contradictory reporting relationships were seemly designed to avoid accountability especially at the higher levels.

Immediately following the disaster a wall of silence was erected within the department. Senior officials before parliamentary committees alluded to an underway internal investigation into the decision-making process leading to the approval of single-person train operation for Montreal, Maine and Atlantic Railway, but attempts to obtain details through access to information came back empty-handed.

However, Transport Canada's governance document, of which I obtained a copy, outlines the bureaucratic chain of command. (It does not appear on the department's website.)

At the top of the bureaucratic hierarchy was the deputy minister, Louis Lévesque. A Harper appointee, Lévesque came to the post in 2012, succeeding Yaprak Baltacıoğlu, who was in charge during the exponential rise in oil-by-rail traffic. Lévesque chaired the Executive Management Committee, the most senior integrated decision-making body at Transport Canada; specifically its "Policy, Programs and Regulations" arm.

The assistant deputy minister of safety and security, Gerard McDonald, reported directly to the deputy minister and to the Executive Management Committee of which he was a member.

The director general of the Rail Safety Directorate, Luc Bourdon, reported to Assistant Deputy Minister McDonald. He too was a member of the Executive Management Committee

The Quebec regional director general, André Lapointe, its senior representative, reported directly to the deputy minister (not to McDonald), and to the Executive Management Committee of which he was also a member.

Both Bourdon and Lapointe shared accountability for the oversight of program and service delivery according to the governance document.

The Quebec regional director, Luciano Martin, was accountable by line authority to the regional director general, Lapointe; and by functional authority to the director general of the Rail Safety Directorate, Bourdon. As noted earlier, he was very concerned about granting Montreal, Maine and Atlantic Railway permission to operate single-person trains given its shoddy safety record, according to email evidence.

Walter Carlson, the director of operations, equipment and engineering within the Rail Safety Directorate, reported to the director general, Bourdon.

According to multiple former insiders, it was Carlson who green lighted single-person train operation permission for Montreal, Maine and Atlantic Railway. A professional engineer, Carlson worked for CP before moving to the Canadian Transport Commission. When it was dismantled in the mid-1980s, Carlson went to Transport Canada. According to sources, Carlson's attitude was that the best thing the regulator could do was get out of the way. He reportedly said the worst decision Transport Canada had ever made was its imposition of sixty-nine conditions that Quebec North Shore and Labrador would have to meet to continue operating single-crew trains. Carlson was one of only two persons at headquarters interviewed by the Sécurité du Québec criminal investigation into Lac-Mégantic. The other was the track director, Daniel Lafontaine.

Carlson told me that it was not a question of actually making the decision to allow Montreal, Maine and Atlantic Railway to proceed with single-person train operation. With exemptions accompanied by strict conditions, such as those applied to the Quebec North Shore and Labrador Railway, no longer necessary under the revised rail operating rules, companies did not need explicit permission. His job was to make sure the company was adhering to the operating rules; that the company's risk assessments and safety management system were in order; and that guidelines were adhered to. Contradicting the damning evidence from Quebec office personnel and subsequent investigations, notably the Transportation Safety Board investigation, Carlson made the determination that Montreal, Maine and Atlantic Railway could operate safely with single-person crews. Besides, he said, the railway had already been operating with single-crew trains from the border to Nantes for a few years, as well as in Maine.

Although Carlson, as the directorate safety expert, was the point person on Montreal, Maine and Atlantic Railway, he was at the bottom rung of the accountability ladder. He was working within an operating framework and rail safety regulatory regime that had previously been approved and put in place by persons well above him in the bureaucratic hierarchy, and ultimately approved by the minister at the time. Furthermore, Carlson's sign-off on the Montreal, Maine and Atlantic Railway file occurred with tacit, if not explicit, concurrence on the part of persons up the convoluted accountability ladder, who chose to ignore the advice of other safety experts within the department, especially the Quebec office.

His immediate boss, Bourdon, another former CP employee, told *Maclean's* days after the crash that the company had demonstrated to Transport Canada that it could operate safely with just one person at the controls.[1] He was very much in the loop in the process leading to Montreal, Maine and Atlantic Railway being given permission to proceed with stage one of its single-person operation initiative in 2010. When Carlson went to Maine to negotiate the extension of single-person train operation with railway executives (Quebec office representatives refused to attend), Bourdon signed his expense claims. After the fact, according to sources, he, remarkably, continued to insist he was not aware Montreal, Maine and Atlantic Railway had proceeded with stage two of its single-person train initiative.

Bourdon's boss, Assistant Deputy Minister Gerard McDonald, was a Harper appointee, and was on board with the government's regulatory and economic priorities. He would most likely have been briefed on discussions and their outcome.

According to sources, the US Federal Railroad Administration, which allowed Montreal, Maine and Atlantic Railway to run its trains in Maine with a single-person crew, was also being briefed on its progress, all the way up to the deputy head of the agency.

André Lapointe, the Quebec regional office director general was aware that his own director, Luciano Martin, had expressed serious reservations. Lapointe reported directly to Deputy Minister Louis Lévesque, not to McDonald. Bourdon and Lapointe were both members of the Executive Management Committee chaired by Lévesque. Presumably, he would have expressed the Quebec region's reservations to Lévesque and the committee.

Montreal, Maine and Atlantic Railway's request to run its trains carrying massively increasing volumes of dangerous cargo through populated areas was precedent setting. The railway was the first freight company seeking to take advantage of the Canadian Rail Operating Rules General Rule M loophole, namely without needing an exemption along with the rigorous conditions that had applied previously. Both the Railway Association and Montreal, Maine and Atlantic Railway owner, Edward Burkhardt, were engaged in a lobbying full court press. Montreal, Maine and Atlantic Railway was a test case for the railways, which wanted to move in this direction.

It stretches credulity that decision-makers right up the chain of command were not aware of the Montreal, Maine and Atlantic Railway request. It stretches credulity that they were not aware of the preconditions outlined by the soon to be released National Research Council report into single-person train operations. It stretches credulity that the single-person operation issue was not raised at the most senior decision-making committee. It stretches credulity to believe higher-ups did not explicitly, or implicitly, give the nod to

Walter Carlson's approval over opposition from Transport Canada's Quebec office.

However, the convoluted governance structure provided protection from direct accountability. Thus, the answer to the question: where did the bureaucratic accountability buck stop? As with ministerial responsibility: nowhere.

In March 2012, not long after the decisive meeting between Montreal, Maine and Atlantic Railway and Transport Canada officials, the National Research Council submitted its single-person train report that Transport Canada had commissioned.[2] The report raised a number of red flags, concluding that, "reducing the train crew to one person without appropriate operational changes and technological intervention diminishes safety."

The report recommended the use of risk-mitigating measures such as an automated warning system, some form of electronic train control and various vigilance devices. It recommended a comprehensive and systematic approach to solo trains, including sustained training, educational programs and specifically designed procedures. It recommended that Transport Canada conduct a two-year test program on a suitable route.

These recommendations were not followed. Montreal, Maine and Atlantic Railway was given permission to proceed in May 2012.

Throughout this period, Transport Canada inspectors continued to identify safety violations at Montreal, Maine and Atlantic Railway. In January 2012, the inspectors issued a "letter of concern" to the railway, stating its employees lacked training to perform inspections and brake-effectiveness tests designed to ensure proper train securement. In February, they issued a notice regarding numerous infractions at the rail traffic control office in Farnham. It found that some rail traffic controllers were not familiar with parts of the Canadian Rail Operating Rules, and that Montreal, Maine and Atlantic Railway had no process in place to ensure compliance with these rules. In April, Transport Canada issued a letter of insufficient action, citing deficiencies in the railway's response to the February notice.

In May, two directions were issued to Montreal, Maine and Atlantic Railway by a Transport Canada health and safety officer for failure to protect employees from workplace hazards under the *Canada Labour Code.*

But none of it stopped the solo train juggernaut.

CHAPTER 6

Harper and Harrison

About the same time Burkhardt was meeting with Transport Canada officials to get the go-ahead for his plan to extend single-person crews, the Harper government — now in a majority position after the May 2011 election — was ramping up its deregulation agenda.

Harper's administration was much less concerned than its predecessors with masking the deregulation agenda in euphemisms such as "smart regulation." Portraying regulations as "job-killing, wealth-destroying red tape," the Harper government launched the Red Tape Reduction Commission in January 2011.[1] The commission was modelled on a project of the Mike Harris Ontario government of the 1990s — a government that shared no less than five cabinet ministers with Harper's and whose own deregulation drive had resulted in the Walkerton tragedy described in Chapter 1.

The Red Tape Reduction Commission's conclusions were incorporated into the government's regulatory policy, which took the form of the Cabinet Directive on Regulatory Management, taking effect in the spring of 2012.[2]

The directive was framed by seven basic principles. Only one specified the need to protect health, safety and the environment. The rest dealt with efficiency, balancing costs and benefits, "sound science," competitiveness, elimination of red tape and transparency. According to a Treasury Board source, costs to business became in practice the sole test for determining whether a proposed regulation was accepted.

Under the directive, building on the previous Liberal regulatory policy, risk-management approaches sidelined the precautionary principle — namely that in the face of scientific uncertainty, regulators should err on the side of caution. Now business-friendly guidelines and voluntary codes were preferred options to actual regulation.[3] According to one expert on regulatory issues, Marc Lee, "The risk-management approach defers judgment unless risks are sufficiently large, based on a rigorous, scientific demonstration of harm. This places the burden of proof in the opposite place — on the regulator."[4] The tack strengthened the ability of companies to use "sound science" arguments to delay or block the introduction of new regulations.

The directive also introduced a life-cycle approach where regulations were re-evaluated every five years — one step short of "sunset clauses," where a regulation automatically expires and has to be rejustified if it is to continue. Centralized screening of regulatory proposals in the Regulatory Affairs Secretariat of the Treasury Board added an extra layer of review and opportunity for industry pushback.

Another roadblock was that proposed regulations had to be screened to ensure their consistency with international trade and investment agreements. Regulations had to pass a necessity test, meaning they must not be more burdensome than necessary to achieve their objectives. This was code for ensuring proposed safety regulations would not be a trade barrier.

Regulations were also screened for possible challenges by foreign-owned corporations, using the investor-state dispute settlement provisions of NAFTA. They created secret arbitration tribunals that allowed companies to circumvent domestic courts to sue governments for policies or regulations they deemed to adversely affect their profits. It gave companies — including the railways — another tool to neutralize regulatory agencies.

The centrepiece of the Harper government's regulatory policy, however, was the "one-for-one" rule, which mandated that regulatory agencies offset each proposed new or amended regulation by removing at least one existing regulation. One-for-one, which came into effect in April 2012, was the key mechanism for implementing the government's little-known "regulatory budget" initiative.

The regulatory budget defined and quantified regulations solely as a cost to business — a "hidden tax." A metric was devised to measure progress, and an external private-sector watchdog committee was established to oversee the process and ensure that bureaucrats did not stonewall the government's agenda. According to former Prime Minister's Office adviser Shawn Speer, Harper personally championed this deregulation initiative. The prime minister's personal involvement sent a powerful message to cabinet ministers and the federal bureaucracy: Resistance would not be tolerated.

Harper patterned his one-for-one approach after British Conservative Prime Minister David Cameron's even more aggressive two-for-one rule. Cameron boasted of running "the first government in modern history that at the end of its parliamentary term has less regulation in place than there was at the beginning." One example of his zeal, eliminating the rule requiring builders to install sprinkler systems in apartments, is now seen as a contributing factor in the 2017 Grenfell Tower fire in London, in which seventy-two people died.

The new regime in Ottawa often put regulators in an impossible quandary.

One source, hired for a Transport Canada research project to ostensibly streamline regulations, was deeply troubled when he came to realize that the real goal was simply to eliminate regulations that, in accordance with Transport Canada's primary mandate, were put in place explicitly to uphold public safety.

The deregulation push was just one element in a suite of Harper government actions to undermine the independence of government agencies. In 2007, Harper fired Linda Keen, the president of the Canadian Nuclear Safety Commission, who defied a government order that she had determined would subordinate public safety to government priorities and industry interests. "It put a chill through the federal system," according to former auditor general Sheila Fraser, whose own appointment was not renewed.[5]

The Conservative government also severed the traditional buffers between itself and the apex of the public service: the Privy Council Office. A highly placed source said, "The co-optation of the Privy Council Office broke its traditional independence. Its new role was to execute the will of the government without question — to carry out government business like good loyal soldiers." The source continued: "The Privy Council Office no longer provided a buffer between the political level and the bureaucratic level. It was thoroughly politicized." A former Public Works official wrote that arm's-length policy advice or evidence-based analysis was disregarded: "No longer do public servants speak knowledge to power. They are expected instead to pander to known, already-made decisions and biases."[6]

BOOSTING OIL BY RAIL

The pillars of the Harper agenda — deregulation and its enabler austerity, making Canada into a petroleum powerhouse — made it hard to see the danger of transporting oil by rail. Rather, the approach was boosterish. A 2012 memo prepared for Natural Resources Minister Joe Oliver highlighted the benefits of transporting oil by rail to tidewater to overcome the price discounting that was disadvantaging Alberta's landlocked oil industry. Natural Resources Canada, it said, "is currently meeting with Transport Canada to mutually understand how rail can be part of a solution to current market access challenges."[7]

Transport Canada, for its part, was complacent about the dangers. A May 2012 internal Transport Canada memo obtained by Greenpeace stated the department had "identified no major safety concerns with the increased oil-by-rail capacity in Canada, nor with the safety of tank cars that are designed, maintained, qualified and used according to Canadian and US standards and regulations. Indeed, Canada and the US work collaboratively to ensure the harmonization of rail safety requirements."[8]

The Conservatives had won their second term in 2008 as the global recession was starting to bite. The opposition parties made it a condition of their support that the government bring in a stimulus package, which the Conservatives did despite their ideological aversion to Keynesian measures. The 2009–10 budget boosted Transport Canada's Rail Safety Directorate spending to $43.8 million. However, the department did not spend the whole amount that year. And over the next four years, in line with the Harper government's austerity initiative, it spent less than budgeted each year. In the fiscal year beginning April 2013, as the oil-by-rail boom was approaching its peak, an already resource-challenged rail safety division actually spent 30 per cent less than what it had been allocated four years earlier.[9]

The Transportation of Dangerous Goods Directorate was aware of possible problems as early as 2009 but lacked the resources to properly inspect the contents of the Bakken oil trains en route. The directorate saw its budget frozen at around $13 to $14 million during this period, which limited inspections to rail-loading terminals. Layoffs and forced retirements drained vital in-house expertise.[10] Asked at a 2014 Transport Committee hearing if there should have been more inspectors, given the increase in the volume of dangerous goods transported by rail, the director general of the Transportation of Dangerous Goods Directorate, Marie-France Dagenais, replied: "I'm not the one who decides that."[11]

As for the Canadian Transportation Agency, charged with ensuring railways had sufficient insurance coverage to cover accidents, it did not have the mandate or the resources to monitor changes, like the sudden shift in Montreal, Maine and Atlantic Railway's cargo from forest products to oil, that would necessitate an increase in its insurance liability. Its modest budget was also frozen during this entire period. The agency simply took the company's word that it was in compliance and did not need a variance to its operating certificate: a pro forma paper exercise. The volume of oil transported by Montreal, Maine and Atlantic Railway had increased by 280 per cent from 2011 to 2012. Its insurance coverage remained at $25 million.

On the Montreal, Maine and Atlantic Railway line and others, trains pulling an uninterrupted string of one hundred or more tank cars, each train carrying up to eighty thousand barrels of oil, had suddenly become commonplace. Yet nowhere within Transport Canada was a global risk assessment taken of the oil-by-rail boom.

WARNINGS DISMISSED

There were, it's true, dissident voices within Transport Canada. But their warnings were generally dismissed.

Internal briefing notes prepared for Transport Minister Denis Lebel after the 2011 election warned that the industry's lobbying against stricter safety regulations was "counter to the public's expectation for strict regulation and zero risk tolerance . . . The current safety oversight system is vulnerable to increases in traffic as the existing suite of policy instruments has limitations and diminishing returns that need to be addressed."[12]

But warnings were easily drowned out. Jean-Pierre Gagnon, an engineer recognized as one of the foremost tank-car experts in North America, had been sounding cautions about the dangers of oil-by-rail for years when he was "retired" by the Harper government. Five engineers who worked alongside him also saw their jobs eliminated. At the time, Gagnon was working on a review of tank cars, including DOT-111s. "My 'retirement' was done entirely for cost reasons. I was a high-priced staff person doing work that was not considered a high priority," Gagnon told me.

On the eve of his departure in March 2013, Gagnon expressed concern about the possibility of a major oil-train accident. He told a *La Presse* reporter: "We're due."

Réjean Simard, a Transport Canada specialist in the Transportation of Dangerous Goods Directorate who, like Gagnon, was "retired," told *Enquête* that there was no congruence between the resources available in the directorate and the huge increase in oil transportation. Simard said he pleaded with his bosses to include crude oil as a dangerous good requiring an emergency response plan, but to no avail. As late as April 2013, Transport Canada had still not made this designation.[13]

Meanwhile, the US Pipeline and Hazardous Materials Safety Administration was recording an alarming rise in oil spilled from derailments: in 2013, almost twice as much had spilled as in the entire previous thirty-five years combined.

A LACK OF RIGOUR AT TRANSPORT CANADA

Besides being under resourced in safety-related areas, as we saw in Chapter 1, research by Anaïs Valiquette L'Heureux found that Transport Canada was a rigidly hierarchical, highly siloed department with poor internal communication and frequent turf wars between policy, operational, regional and safety divisions, as well as between headquarters and regional offices. L'Heureux called it "organizational narcissism." The dysfunction was blinding senior officials to the growing dangers posed by the oil-by-rail boom.

A December 2011 report from the environmental commissioner in the auditor general's office warned Transport Canada that it was not adequately enforcing rules to prevent spills of dangerous goods.[14] The report found that the department's Transportation of Dangerous Goods Directorate did not know which companies handled dangerous goods, nor did it prioritize inspections based on an overall risk assessment strategy. The commissioner's sample of the directorate's inspections revealed that in instances where inspections found a company to be non-compliant with federal regulations, almost three-quarters of these showed incomplete or no evidence of follow-up by the directorate to ensure corrective action had been taken.

Transport Canada promised to implement the environment commissioner's recommendations. But by April 2013, it still had not fully complied with key recommendations aimed at improving inspections and compliance. A Transport Canada spokesperson told reporter Mike De Souza that the department had been granted an extension by the auditor general. The claim was repudiated by a spokesperson from the auditor general: "We aren't, as auditors, the ones who grant extensions. That is Transport Canada's own decision, for which they alone are accountable."[15]

Like its environment commissioner, the office of the auditor general found Transport Canada lacking in rigour. In a 2013 report, it said the department had conducted just 26 per cent of its planned safety management system audits over a three-year period to March 2012, and only 10 per cent of its rail safety inspectors were qualified to carry out the audits.

Moreover, in the large majority of cases where safety management system audits were conducted, there was no follow-up by inspectors to ensure that corrective actions had actually been taken. Transport Canada, it also found, did not do a proper analysis to determine its overall needs for implementing the safety management system regime: how many inspectors, how many auditors, how much training and how many resources it needed to do the job. Nor were Transport Canada's own risk assessments taking into account future risks that the industry might face, such as the increase in the transportation of dangerous goods. The report concluded: "The department's level of oversight was not sufficient to obtain assurance that federal railways have implemented adequate and effective safety management systems."

Transport Canada's enforcement tools were weak, as were penalties for non-compliance. Under Section 31 of the *Railway Safety Act*, rail safety inspectors could issue various warnings. In order of increasing severity, these were a letter of non-compliance, a letter of concern, a notice and a "notice and order."

However, rail safety inspectors were reluctant to start an enforcement action. The burden of proof was on inspectors. According to a former insider, inspectors were judged on the number of orders they did *not* issue. He told me: "Every regional Transport Canada safety inspector or manager knows he is putting his career on the line every time he signs a notice and order on an issue that the railway is prepared to defend to the legal limit and beyond."

The minister of transport had the power under Section 32 of the *Railway Safety Act* to issue a ministerial order, though such orders are subject to complicated appeal procedures, and an order is automatically stayed if the company appeals it.[16] The minister also had the power to issue a court order. Yet there is no evidence such actions were made, even in the case of a serial offender like Montreal, Maine and Atlantic Railway.

Overall, the laissez-faire culture lulled the industry and regulators into complacency, even as skyrocketing oil shipments increased the likelihood of such an accident. The railway lobby never let up in Ottawa. During the years of the oil-by-rail boom — January 1, 2009, to August 31, 2013 — submissions to the commissioner of lobbying indicate that CN lobbyists had 521 "communications" with government or parliamentary officials, 210 of which were with Transport Canada. CP registered 121 communications, of which forty-one were with Transport Canada. And the Railway Association of Canada registered sixty-eight such communications. Their explicit purpose reported to the commissioner of lobbying was to argue that there was no need for any new regulations.

And the same message was promoted in other spheres. CN CEO Claude Mongeau told a 2012 Wall Street analysts briefing: "If you have one railcar that gets punctured, it is 600 barrels that might spill . . . [This is] nothing like what could happen if you have a spill with a pipeline."

HUNTER HARRISON RETURNS TO CENTRE STAGE

A series of US regulatory changes in the 1990s transformed the ability of hedge fund investors — despite holding a small minority of a targeted company's shares — to wield enormous power over its activities, with the singular goal of extracting shareholder value.[17] In the railway industry, the gold-standard measure for boosting shareholder value for these so-called activist investors became the operating ratio — the relationship of operating costs to revenue.

In this light, it was natural that CP caught the eye of Bill Ackman, a hedge-fund manager who had established the New York–based Pershing Square Capital Management fund in 2004. When Ackman began buying CP shares in 2011, the company's operating ratio was 90 per cent, the highest in the industry. It was like a beacon to the sort of investor who specialized in shakeups, which in turn goosed share prices.

Ackman also saw CP's potential as a transporter of Bakken shale and Alberta bitumen as the oil-by-rail boom was ramping up.

Ackman's choice of shakeup agent was none other than Hunter Harrison, whom he lured out of retirement. Ackman then challenged the incumbent management by initiating a proxy war, driving up CP's share price by 60 per cent and acquiring more than 12 per cent of its shares. Ackman demanded several board seats and CEO Fred Green's resignation.

The board, familiar with Harrison's reputation at CN, including his record of alienating customers, unanimously opposed Ackman's demands. However, a number of institutional investors, notably the Ontario Teachers Pension Fund and the Canada Pension Plan Investment Board, attracted by the prospect of higher returns, supported Ackman's board slate at the May 2012 proxy vote. Ackman's victory forced the resignation of Green and CP's entire board. Harrison was installed as CEO.

As we've seen, CP, now headquartered in Calgary, with close business and cultural ties to the petroleum industry and a vast North American rail network linked to the oil sands, was well-positioned to take advantage of the bitumen boom. CP had begun experimenting with oil-by-rail in 2009. In 2011, it hauled thirteen thousand carloads.

With more track in North Dakota than any other operator except Burlington Northern Santa Fe, CP was also well-placed to haul shale oil from there.

Indeed, oil and railway industries in both regions formed a seamless web from wellhead to market, with a common stake in the unconventional oil production boom.

One of the first things Harrison did was to remove the iconic beaver from CP's logo — a symbol of its historical role. He did not waste any time in applying his "precision railroading" formula from his days at CN: revamping scheduling practices, reducing the number of trains and increasing their size and speed, running trains with inadequately trained engineers, ditching locomotives and unprofitable customers, slashing costs and workforce. Harrison told the *Financial Post*, "I kind of went through Canada maybe like Sherman went through Atlanta." Complaints from Western grain farmers against CP's revamped scheduling practices led the government to impose minimum ship-ment requirements on the company.[18]

Harrison had no time for the idea that these changes compromised safety. He told shareholders that speed had nothing to do with the number or severity of oil-train derailments and that greater velocity was the key to future growth and profits. During his time at CP, Harrison increased the number of cars per train by 24 per cent and shrunk its workforce, according to one set of figures, from 19,500 to 11,700.

Though CP profited immensely from transporting crude oil, Harrison cynically talked out of both sides of his mouth. One day he was saying he wanted his company out of the oil transportation business, casting his company as a reluctant shipper of oil, a hostage to it. The next he was dispatching his lobbyists to Washington to push back against new oil train regulations such as speed limitations, which might reduce the profitability of this lucrative revenue source.

To the delight of CP's shareholders, profits and share prices soared as CP's operating ratio plummeted. Oil volumes more than doubled to seventy thousand carloads by 2013.[19] In the first two years under Harrison, CP stock prices soared from $75 to $242 per share in October 2014.

As at CN, Harrison had a fractious relationship with workers and unions.[20] During his watch, there were two major strikes. Firings, disciplinary actions, union grievances and arbitrations skyrocketed. The culture inculcated by Harrison included a fear of reporting problems. One worker who was fired for allegedly not following procedure on injury reporting told the *Globe and Mail*, "Now everyone is terrified to report any injuries or illnesses . . . Everyone is scared to book off when they're tired, because they could get fired for it."

Doug Finnson, head of the Teamsters Canada Rail Conference, put Harrison's anti-union methodology in a nutshell: "Tie up the union defending rights they already have so their demands at the bargaining table will likely be limited to resolving the outstanding disputes." As at CN, Harrison expanded training of managers and other non-union staff so they could double as locomotive engineers and conductors as needed, including in the event of a strike. Many of these staff were reluctant, and some were terrified, but they felt they had no choice in the matter.

The Transportation Safety Board expressed concern that inadequately trained employees were hauling dangerous goods through the challenging terrain of British Columbia after an incident in Cranbrook.[21] But Harrison revelled in the culture of fear he brought to CP. He told *Globe and Mail* reporter Eric Atkins: "You can call it fear or accountability, responsibility, whatever, but it is just basic. The hard part is that someone created a culture of permissiveness, which means that somebody else has to make a change."

Harrison, of course, was no fan of regulation, believing the government's role was to basically get out of the way and let the railways run their business. His view fit well with the Harper government's deregulation agenda. For example, a Harper omnibus budget bill provision replaced Transportation Safety Board mandatory accident reporting regulations with non-binding voluntary guidelines. This allowed Harrison to use this loophole to inaccurately declare a major reduction in CP's accidents in subsequent years.

From the time Harrison took over as head of CP in 2012, its net income rose from $484 million to $1.6 billion in 2016. Even with the collapse of oil and other resource prices, it was still around $150 per share by August 2016, the month Pershing Square's Ackman cashed out his remaining shares, pocketing an estimated $2.6 billion net profit from his five-year adventure with CP.

During that period, shareholders realized an annual return of over 45 per cent. The company's operating ratio fell from the highest in the business to the lowest, from 90 per cent to just under 60 per cent.[22] In 2016, his last year at CP, Harrison took home in compensation — base salary plus bonus, plus share-based compensation, plus option-based and other compensation — $18,829,794: the fifth-highest-paid CEO in Canada.[23]

While the shareholders got rich, workers and the public as a whole were put in danger. In 2014, even a compliant Transport Canada imposed an unprecedented order on CP, demanding the company change its fatigue-management practices in British Columbia, which were adversely affecting the alertness of train crews hauling dangerous goods and posed "an immediate threat to safe railway operations."

TIPPING POINT

In the spring of 2012, Irving Oil decided to buy Bakken crude for its Saint John refinery. Despite the additional transportation costs, this option was now cheaper than buying oil from sources abroad like the North Sea. The transportation job was contracted to CP.

CP, however, no longer had track all the way to Saint John, which meant it had to choose another line to subcontract with: either CN, whose line hugged the south shore of the St. Lawrence River, or the shorter Montreal, Maine and Atlantic Railway route through Maine.

Montreal, Maine and Atlantic Railway was chosen because it was the cheaper option. Irving was on board, since this option required that its own New Brunswick Southern Railway would carry the oil on the last leg of the last leg, so to speak, from Maine to Saint John.

It was a win-win-win situation, except for one problem. It was incumbent on CP, in accordance with risk assessment obligations, under its safety management system, to select the route with that minimized safety risks. But Montreal, Maine and Atlantic Railway had a poor safety record. And now, with Transport Canada's blessing, it would be running these giant oil trains along a poorly maintained track, using shoddy locomotives. And with a single operator.

CHAPTER 7
Eve of Destruction

A railroader from a family of railroaders, Tom Harding, Jr., joined CP in 1980 at the age of eighteen. After CP sold the Mégantic line in 1995, he stayed on with a succession of owners, the last of them arriving in 2003, when Montreal, Maine and Atlantic Railway was formed.

Harding, who turned fifty-three in 2013, grew up and still resides in Farnham, a railway town south of Montreal at the entrance to the Eastern Townships. A passionate hockey player in his youth, Harding eventually gave up hockey for the less demanding sport of snowboarding. He was immensely proud of his son, who had just graduated from Bishop's College School in Lennoxville, Quebec. Lately, much of the elder Harding's days were taken up caring for his ailing mother.

For more than two years, he had been driving the Lac-Mégantic route, a shift that deposited him in the town overnight. Harding usually stayed at an inn called l'Eau Berge, along with the American crew who would take the train across the border the next morning.

Lac-Mégantic had become his second home. Staff and bar regulars at the inn described him as kind and friendly, game to chat in accented French. Gilles Fluet, who talked regularly with Harding, said he never stayed for more than a beer after his shift. Harding and the other Montreal, Maine and Atlantic Railway drivers would often complain about the poor condition of the company's locomotives.

Harding was respected by fellow workers. He was an exception to Montreal, Maine and Atlantic Railway's culture of negligence, according to his former colleague, Kevin Mosher. "He was knowledgeable about the rules and always applied them. He was one the few employees at Montreal, Maine and Atlantic Railway who always diligently applied himself to his work," says Mosher. Another former colleague, conductor Jonathan Couture, described Harding as patient and safety-conscious.

Couture recalled an incident when he and Harding, as a crew, were bound for Lac-Mégantic. They were leaving the Sherbrooke yard when Couture realized he was not sure he had applied the handbrakes on the cars they had left in the yard. "I decided to speak to Tom about it before we were too far," Couture said, "His reaction was to stop the train and ask me to go back. Tom told me that my conscience should dictate my moves."

CLEAR WARNINGS
In July 2012, Irving Oil started doing a few test runs with Bakken oil. The same month, Montreal, Maine and Atlantic Railway began operating its trains with a single operator, without providing advance notice to Transport Canada as it had promised. (Other than a few test runs, Irving Oil didn't start hauling Bakken crude via Montreal, Maine and Atlantic Railway until November 2012.)

In starting up the new system, Montreal, Maine and Atlantic Railway did not abide by its intention, as stated to Transport Canada, to decrease train length from one hundred cars to fifty for single-person trains, or to improve track conditions to enhance safety and allow engineers to reach their destination sooner, thereby reducing the risk of fatigue.

Although Montreal, Maine and Atlantic Railway's safety management systems plan called for four hours of training for locomotive engineers to adjust to not having a second crew member, training consisted of a twenty-minute briefing in the manager's office. Harding's training was delivered within the hour preceding his first departure. In contrast, Quebec North Shore and Labrador had a thousand-hour training program for its lone engineers driving its decidedly lower-risk iron ore trains in lower-risk northern Quebec.

Contrary to its safety management systems documents, Montreal, Maine and Atlantic Railway undertook no job-task analysis for a single-person crew, nor any analysis of potential hazards associated with those tasks. Montreal, Maine and Atlantic Railway did not do a risk assessment of the safety implications of leaving parked trains unattended on the steeply sloped main track at Nantes. The railway did not consider Nantes a high-risk location in its safety management system.

But for that matter, senior Transport Canada officials also thought a new risk assessment was unnecessary. Meanwhile the department's Transportation of Dangerous Goods Directorate was not verifying the accuracy of the Bakken train's volatility classification documents, either through testing en route or at the Irving refinery.

Transport Canada had 102 rail safety personnel, fifteen in Quebec. It had thirty-five dangerous goods inspectors in 2013, only sixteen of whom were qualified for rail, and none were specifically assigned to Quebec. These numbers had not changed since at least 2004.[1] In 2009, there was the equivalent of fourteen carloads of crude oil per dangerous goods inspector. By 2013, that ratio had increased to about 4,500 carloads per inspector.[2]

Transport Canada's Quebec regional office had only two operations inspectors to do on-site inspections for the entire provincial network. A former insider told me: "If we don't get specific complaints, we cannot take action. We were not aware Montreal, Maine and Atlantic Railway was leaving trains on the main track at Nantes. To our knowledge, they were on the siding protected by an exemption derail" (a device that can be set to stop a train from moving).

The Quebec office conducted a limited safety management system audit of Montreal, Maine and Atlantic Railway in October 2012, which discovered a number of deficiencies, as well as the company's failure to report four accidents. The Transportation Safety Board investigation into the Lac-Mégantic disaster revealed that Montreal, Maine and Atlantic Railway had not reported twenty-two accidents from 2007 to 2013. While the railway did submit a corrective action plan to Transport Canada, most of its safety management system deficiencies were never resolved.

In November 2012, Irving began receiving large quantities of Bakken oil using the CP–Montreal, Maine and Atlantic Railway route. Between November and July 6, 2013, Montreal, Maine and Atlantic Railway hauled sixty-seven trains with a total of 3,830 tank cars laden with Bakken crude. The lone crew member parked these trains on the main track, unattended, at Nantes, on top of a hill that sloped down steeply toward the heart of Lac-Mégantic eleven kilometres away.

It had now become a deadly game of Russian roulette: not if, but when.

The same month oil trains began rolling, Lac-Mégantic town council sent a letter to Transport Minister Denis Lebel and the local Conservative member of Parliament, Christian Paradis, warning them about the poor condition of Montreal, Maine and Atlantic Railway's track, in particular an unstable section of track embankment at the north end of town that tended to be eroded by heavy rain. The letter read, in part: "A train derailment containing toxic products or contaminants at this location is likely to cause considerable damage, considering the proximity to residences."

Montreal, Maine and Atlantic Railway had tried to fix the problem over several years but it kept recurring. After being contacted by Transport Canada, it went through this procedure once again. A Transport Canada inspector verified that the work had been done.

In early 2013, inspectors from Transport Canada's Transportation of Dangerous Goods Directorate found improperly classified oil on a CP train. However, when they alerted the company, the train had already departed eastward. There was no follow-up by officials.

NO NEW RULES

There were no fiery oil train derailments involving either Bakken oil or Alberta bitumen in the months preceding Lac-Mégantic. There were, however, warning signs. Between March and May 2013, CP had several small oil spills in Northern Ontario, Saskatchewan and Minnesota. The largest of these was an accident near Parkers Prairie, Minnesota, involving a train hauling ninety-four cars. Fourteen cars derailed and three ruptured, spilling 115,000 litres of Alberta bitumen.

Discussing these cases, CP spokespeople generally dismissed the idea that they posed a danger to the public, repeating standard talking points, mantra-like, about the stellar safety record of CP and the industry as a whole.

In fact, the railways seemed indifferent to the danger. In the six months leading up to the Lac-Mégantic disaster, industry lobbyists repeatedly petitioned politicians and bureaucrats, insisting that strengthened regulations to cope with the burgeoning oil-by-rail boom were unnecessary. At times they argued for existing regulations to be removed.

The Railway Association of Canada, which was once a repository of substantial technical expertise, had become almost exclusively a lobbying organization. A consummate lobbyist — and non-railroader — took the helm as CEO in April 2012. Michael Bourque had worked in the Privy Council Office under Brian Mulroney and later for a big pharma company and the Chemical Association of Canada. The Railway Association's attempt to forestall tighter regulation was recorded in Ottawa's Registry of Lobbyists for the period January 1 to July 8, 2013. The association aimed, it said, "To inform about the movement of dangerous goods, including voluntary and regulatory requirements, volumes, customers and safety measures to assure [the federal government] that current regulations for dangerous goods transportation are sufficient."[3]

CP lobbyists met with advisers to Transport Minister Lebel in April 2013. The subject and purpose, among others, was "Transport Canada's review of freight rail service in Canada . . . advocating for no additional regulation." CN's manager of safety and regulatory affairs, Sam Berrada, appeared before the Senate Energy, Environment and Natural Resources Committee in May. When asked whether Transport Canada should hire more inspectors, Berrada said: "There is no further requirement for Transport Canada to do any more than what they currently do."[4]

Nevertheless, the oil-by-rail phenomenon had caught the attention of the International Energy Agency, which released a report in May warning that even though spill volumes were higher for pipelines than railways, the surge in oil-by-rail traffic raised safety questions.

CBC investigative reporters Dave Seglins and John Nicol revealed that on June 7, 2013, the Railway Association had asked Lebel to strike the operating rule that required certified railcar inspectors conduct detailed examinations of tank cars carrying dangerous goods before they were loaded.

The railway unions opposed this proposed change. Unifor's Brian Stevens wrote to the Railway Association to say that its risk assessment was incomplete and that the measures proposed to mitigate risk were insufficient. Specifically, Stevens said the association's proposal to replace on-site inspectors with wayside scanner technology was unproven, ineffective and "not in the public interest." Teamsters representative Robert Smith responded in the same vein, while also pointing out the obvious: that the transportation of oil by rail had suddenly increased massively. "This is therefore not the time to be considering a relaxation of rules . . . but rather a time to maintain that which is in place to safeguard these increased movements."[5]

There were no signs of apprehension among senior management at Transport Canada, whose officials later told *Globe and Mail* reporter Grant Robertson that they had not been aware of the alarm bells raised by the Federal Railroad Administration earlier in the year — that some Bakken crude was highly explosive and was not being labelled properly. The Railway Safety Directorate later claimed that it was only made aware of the dangers a few months before the disaster. But this is belied by warnings that had been made by Transport Canada experts Rejean Simard and Jean-Pierre Gagnon.

Long-overdue amendments to the *Railway Safety Act*, legislated in May 2013, promised additional enforcement tools — the ability to levy fines on railways and suspend their operating certificates for safety violations. But the regulations putting these amendments into force were not yet in place. That same month, Transport Canada inspectors reported more safety violations at Montreal, Maine and Atlantic Railway.

Communities along the Montreal, Maine and Atlantic Railway route from Farnham to Lac-Mégantic were unnerved by the sudden appearance of enormous oil trains rolling through their neighbourhoods. Some mayors, apprehensive about one-person crews, contacted Transport Canada. Montreal, Maine and Atlantic Railway was by now hauling two unit trains per week laden with Bakken crude. The mayor of Farnham, Josef Hüsler, later told Radio Canada's *Enquête* that runaway cars had become a regular occurrence in his town. "They have never invested money . . . And the rails are not getting better. How is it that they can keep operating?" Lac-Mégantic's environment officer, Robert Mercier, said his office attempted to raise questions with the railway. "It was a great concern about the train and the condition of the rail and all these tank cars that were passing every day," he said. Nantes Fire Chief Patrick Lambert, whose team had put out several fires on Montreal, Maine and Atlantic Railway trains over the previous eight years, worried about the absence of buffer cars that might limit the spread of a fire following a derailment.

Across the border in Hermon, Maine, where Montreal, Maine and Atlantic Railway was headquartered, a citizens group set up a blockade in mid-June, preventing trains from passing through town. Police disbanded the group and arrested some of its members. Later in the month, another group blocked the tracks in Fairfield belonging to Pan Am Railways, the other line besides Montreal, Maine and Atlantic Railway carrying Bakken crude through the state.

The Bakken crude that Irving had been receiving since the previous November had typically been labelled with the lowest volatility classification, PG III ("PG" stands for "packing group"). The law allowed

Irving, as refiner, to simply rely on the shipper's classification. But Irving had been sending back the empty railcars, which contained crude residue, only after changing the classification to the most hazardous level, PG I.

In June, Irving raised concerns about the volatility and misclassification of the oil it was receiving. At an industry conference on June 6, 2013, Irving's quality control manager, Gary Weimer, said the rail-to-refinery system was relying too much on testing tank-car contents only after they had arrived at their destination, which was too late in the process to address any safety issues. Testing at the Irving refinery, moreover, revealed that tank cars contained "sludge," "contaminants" and "unknown substances." Worried about what was going on at the other end in North Dakota, Irving officials urged that more testing be done to protect employees.

In mid-June, a Montreal, Maine and Atlantic Railway train derailed and spilled 13,000 litres of diesel fuel on a remote section of track near the town of Frontenac, adjoining Lac-Mégantic to the southeast. A segment of rail had punctured the tank car containing the train's fuel supply.

Then, on June 27, 2013, a CP train loaded with sixty-two tank cars was crossing the Bonnybrook Bridge in southeast Calgary when the bridge, which belonged to CP, collapsed, leaving six tank cars suspended over the Bow River. Five were carrying volatile diluent used to make bitumen flow. Fortunately, none of the cars spilled or fell into the river, but it was a harrowing experience for Calgarians as rescuers fought to remove the cars from the bridge. It later emerged that CP had not tested the bridge.

FINAL HOURS: NEW TOWN TO NANTES

The ill-fated cargo, loaded onto a seventy-eight-car unit oil train operated by CP, left New Town, North Dakota, on June 30, 2013. Its destination was the Irving Oil refinery in Saint John, New Brunswick, some five thousand kilometres away.

Irving had contracted with World Fuels Services Corp. to provide the oil, which the latter company assembled from eleven local producers and shipped via its subsidiary, Western Petroleum. CP would transport it to Montreal, where it would be transferred to Montreal, Maine and Atlantic Railway for the trip to Maine. At Brownsville Junction, another short-line railroad would transport the train to the New Brunswick border, where the cargo would be picked up by the Irving-owned railway, New Brunswick Southern, for the final leg of its journey to Saint John.

The crude oil was transported from the wellhead by truck to the Dakota Plains loading terminal. The oil was classified as high-volatility flammable liquid: PG I or PG II — though not as a result of actual testing.[6]

Classification rules were lax at the terminal, which was operated by a firm called Strobel Starostka Transfer. The company's standard procedure, it later said, involved conducting a monthly test of a composite sample of crude oil brought to the facility. On the basis of this test, it assigned a classification number to all oil shipments over the following month. Thus, Strobel Starostka switched the Lac-Mégantic-bound shipment to a low-volatility classification, PG III.

The crude was loaded onto standard DOT-111 tank cars leased by Western Petroleum and connected to CP locomotives. The shipping document provided to Western Petroleum by Strobel Starostka — specifying the relationship between the shipping, transporting and purchasing companies — confirmed the oil now had a low-volatility PG III classification. The lawyer who signed the shipping document on behalf of Western Petroleum attested to the accuracy of this classification, though his company had not tested this cargo either. The shipping document was then handed over to CP for the journey east.

From New Town, the train arrived later that night at the CP train yard in Harvey, North Dakota, for its first inspection. It then travelled through Minneapolis, Milwaukee, Chicago and Detroit. It entered Canada at Windsor, winding its way through Ontario towns and cities, including Toronto, along the St. Lawrence River to its final destination: CP's Côte St.-Luc train yard in the heart of Montreal. Still, the crude blew through unencumbered by safety concerns. No tests were done by Transport Canada to verify the volatility of its contents. One car was removed because of mechanical defects that were discovered shortly after departure; five more were removed in Montreal for the same reason.

On the morning of July 5, Montreal, Maine and Atlantic Railway picked up the train in Montreal and transported it along CP tracks to Farnham, just south of Montreal.

At 1:48 p.m., the train departed Farnham. It was 1.4 kilometres long and weighed 10,290 tonnes. It was made up of lead locomotive 5017, four trailing locomotives, a VB car (a caboose equipped to remotely control the locomotives), a buffer car full of sand and seventy-two DOT-111 tank cars loaded with Bakken crude oil. Inspectors from both Transport Canada and Montreal, Maine and Atlantic Railway had examined the tank cars, finding minor problems, but they did not examine the locomotives.

The train's lone operator was Tom Harding. He had agreed to work on his day off because the Montreal, Maine and Atlantic Railway was short of qualified engineers. Harding received a call from a company official at 9:30 a.m. informing him that the scheduled departure time was 1 p.m.

Harding replied that he needed an extra half-hour to run errands for his mother. He asked the rail traffic controller, Steve Jacques, if he would be working with a conductor. (Like air traffic controllers, rail traffic controllers are responsible for co-ordinating safe and efficient operations within a specified territory.) The answer from Jacques was no. As the train was preparing to leave, Jacques asked Montreal, Maine and Atlantic Railway inspector Yves Gendreau, "Are the locomotives okay?"

"Everything is excellent," said Gendreau.

"It's all green, Tom," said Gendreau to Harding.

But the engines were not "excellent." Eight months earlier, locomotive 5017 had been sent to the company's repair shop following an engine failure. A stopgap repair with glue was made to stop an oil leak in the engine block. The repair eventually failed, and the engine repeatedly surged and smoked, causing, among other things, an accumulation of oil in the turbocharger and exhaust manifold.

The day before Harding's fateful trip, another locomotive engineer, François Daigle, who had driven locomotive 5017 to Farnham, noticed it was losing speed and emitting black smoke.

Daigle reported the problem to his supervisor, operations director Jean Demaître, and sent a fax outlining the problem to the repair shop in Derby, Maine. But the shop was closed for the July 4 holiday.

Daigle also asked Demaître if locomotive 5017 could be moved out of the lead position. But that decision was up to the executives in Maine. That spelled a delay of thirty or forty minutes. It was too much time to lose. Demaître dismissed Daigle's request, adding, "You're complaining again."

Daigle later testified in court that the maximum allowable train weight allowed by Montreal, Maine and Atlantic Railway during this period was 6,300 tonnes. But employees were not allowed to refuse overweight trains. Senior Montreal, Maine and Atlantic Railway executives made all the decisions about the length and weight of trains from their offices in Maine. The train that left Farnham on July 5 weighed 9,100 tonnes (both measurements exclude the locomotives). Before the train departed, Transport Canada inspector Alain Richer inspected the cars but not the locomotives.

If the track were well-maintained, the two-hundred-kilometre journey to Nantes would have taken take four to five hours. But it was not well-maintained, a situation Transport Canada had addressed by imposing a speed limit of ten to fifteen miles per hour in the worst parts of the route.

Harding, who had not been informed of the earlier problems on locomotive 5017, reported, minutes after leaving Farnham, that the lead locomotive was surging, and spewing smoke and oil droplets. Harding told Jacques, the Montreal, Maine and Atlantic Railway traffic controller, that his train was moving at only twelve miles per hour: "With five locomotives, I should be doing twenty-two or twenty-three miles per hour."

Harding's trip took almost ten and a half hours.

At 11 p.m. on a gentle midsummer night, Harding parked the train on the main track at the top of the hill above Lac-Mégantic. Parking the train further back on a flatter surface would have blocked a level crossing, which was prohibited by Transport Canada. As far as it may have been from the heights of British Columbia, the final part of the track slope was among the steepest in Canada. In the words of Transportation Safety Board investigator Ian Perkins, it was one of the country's most at-risk locations, though never identified as such by Montreal, Maine and Atlantic Railway.

A less risky location existed at Vachon, on the other side of Lac-Mégantic. But using it would have meant that Harding would have exceeded the allowable maximum of twelve hours on duty.

Before he left the train, Harding contacted the rail traffic controller Dave Wiley in Maine and told him he had turned off four of the five locomotives and applied the handbrakes. The company's operating instructions required that if a train were to be left unattended, the engineer was to leave one locomotive running and its air brake applied. These steps, in combination with handbrakes, constituted a common method for securing trains. But the approach did not conform with the Canadian Rail Operating Rules.

Harding told the Maine controller, "But I have to tell you, I worked it pretty damn hard . . . I've been here ten minutes maybe; it's smoking excessively now, going back and forth, black smoke, and changes to white sometimes."

Wiley, the rail traffic controller, responded: "That's all we can do, Tom. We'll check it in the morning, diagnose it."

They faced a dilemma. If every one of the locomotives were turned off, American regulations required that an air brake test be performed when they were reactivated the next morning — a time-consuming procedure. On the other hand, leaving the locomotive running, despite its mechanical problems, would break one of Montreal, Maine and Atlantic Railway's safety rules.

It was with the company's aversion to delays in mind that Wiley made his decision. There was no discussion of turning on one of the other locomotives.

Leaving trains unattended was normal practice for the industry and is permitted by Transport Canada. Given the train's length, the top of the hill was the only place in Nantes the train could be left overnight without blocking a crossing.

Harding could have parked on a siding at the top of the hill but for three factors. The first was that Montreal, Maine and Atlantic Railway rented it to local particleboard company Tafisa to store empty flat cars. The siding had a derail device to prevent trains from moving. The main track did not.

Montreal, Maine and Atlantic Railway did not inform Transport Canada that it was parking trains on the main track. Engineer Kevin Mosher, who left Montreal, Maine and Atlantic Railway in August 2012, later testified that when he parked trains at Nantes, he always left them on the siding.

So when did that practice change? Likely when Montreal, Maine and Atlantic Railway began to haul oil trains, which were too long to fit on the siding: the second factor. In any case, the siding was in too poor condition to support such heavy trains: the third factor.

What is the right number of handbrakes to apply to secure a seventy-four-car, five-locomotive train that stretches over 1.4 kilometres? However many are applied, it involves a lot of climbing and leveraging — tough physical work, especially for someone at the end of a long solo shift.

The relevant Canadian Rail Operating Rule 112 stated only that "a sufficient number of handbrakes" need be applied, and left it up to individual companies to prescribe the actual number. CP's instructions, for example, specified that eighteen handbrakes be applied in the situation Harding faced. Montreal, Maine and Atlantic Railway's instructions for a train of this many cars, without mentioning slope variations, specified only nine handbrakes, a number arrived at using the "10 per cent plus two" formula, i.e., apply handbrakes on 10 per cent of the cars plus another two.

Canadian Rail Operating Rule 112 required that the operator test the handbrakes while all the air brakes were turned off to ensure the train was secure. But this was not standard practice at Montreal, Maine and Atlantic Railway.

Normally, with a two-person crew, the engineer would conduct a pull-push manoeuvre to stretch and release the couplings between the wagons. Standing outside the train, the conductor would verify that the couplings responded well to the test, and would then apply the handbrakes on the cars. A discussion would ensue between the two about how many handbrakes to apply.

But this option was not available to Harding, and company instructions did not have a communication protocol mandating that the rail traffic controller ask this question to the engineer to compensate for the fact that there was no longer a second crew member. Nor was such a protocol required by Transport Canada as a condition of granting permission to Montreal, Maine and Atlantic Railway for single-person train operations. The Farnham rail traffic controller, Richard Labrie, who had begun his night shift at 6 p.m., did not ask this question to Harding before he left.

Harding applied seven handbrakes, securing the five locomotives, the buffer car and the VB car. Assistant operations director Michael Horan had earlier received an email from his Maine supervisor, Paul Budge, asking him to remind Harding not to set so many handbrakes, as he was in the habit of doing.

Harding performed an efficiency test. However, he did not follow Canadian Rail Operating Rule 112, and shut down the two air brake systems — on the locomotive and on the cars — during the test to ensure the handbrakes could hold the train on their own.

On this point, the Transportation Safety Board investigation into the Lac-Mégantic disaster would conclude that Montreal, Maine and Atlantic Railway's training was woefully inadequate and contrary to all guidelines. Horan, the assistant operations director, would testify that while he was technically responsible for training, he had no formal training in safety education, nor any budget for it.

The Crown's expert witness at the eventual criminal trial resulting from Lac-Mégantic, Steve Callaghan, testified that Harding would have had to apply fourteen handbrakes to keep the train from running away without the backup of the locomotive air brake. The Transportation Safety Board report estimated between eighteen and twenty-six handbrakes would have been needed to hold the train. However, with the locomotive running and its air brake applied along with seven handbrakes, the train was secured with at least twice the retarding force needed to hold the train when Harding left.

Harding could have applied a second air brake system, on the tank cars, before leaving the train. But he was prohibited by the company instructions from doing so because it would take the next locomotive engineer up to an hour to disengage the system the following morning — too costly a delay, in the company's eyes.

Harding had actually been in the habit of applying the automatic brake on the cars to secure the train. But in another email, supervisor Budge asked Horan to remind Harding of the company instructions. (The Transportation Safety Board report would conclude that if the automatic brake had been applied, even with the locomotive brake disabled, it would have held the train likely until the following morning.)[7]

Transport Canada either expressly allowed this practice at Montreal, Maine and Atlantic Railway or simply failed to notice it. In the US, applying the automatic brake is a widely used backup precaution when leaving a train unattended.

Harding left for l'Eau Berge in Lac-Mégantic at 11:30 p.m. He had been awake for almost eighteen hours. André Turcotte, the taxi driver who picked him up, observed smoke coming from the locomotive and oil droplets on the windshield of his car. Turcotte asked Harding whether the train should be left this way. "The company told me to let the engine run," said Harding, who was worried about the possibility of a fire with the engine running. "If the oil level becomes too low, the engine will stop."

Harding was still worried about it, though: "Perhaps I should call the American side," he told Turcotte. "They are more demanding and they might give me other instructions." He wanted to "confirm if he had the right directives," specifically whether it was a good idea to leave a defective locomotive running and unattended.

Ten minutes later, the Nantes fire department received a 911 call reporting a fire on one of the parked Montreal, Maine and Atlantic Railway locomotives. Passerby Denis Claude Vallée shot a video of a pulsing flame shooting out of the locomotive. The flame in the stack was pulsing in sync to the rhythmic growl of the engine. The belching flame eerily lit up the forest behind.

The video showed the arrival of firefighters. They shot water onto the blaze, which only seemed to make it grow. Since neither water nor foam were working, one of the firefighters pushed the emergency button located on the side of the locomotive, which shut down the engine and immediately extinguished the fire. It was midnight.

Locomotive 5017 had been retrofitted and wired differently from most other locomotives. Thus, it did not, unlike the other locomotives on the convoy, have an auto-start penalty brake system. If it had, an automatic penalty brake application on all the cars would have kicked in a few minutes after the engine was shut down, while there was still enough air pressure in the system to prevent movement.

The Sûreté du Québec contacted the rail traffic controller on duty, Richard Labrie, and Montreal, Maine and Atlantic Railway track and signals director Daniel Aubé, informing them of the locomotive fire. Labrie alerted Montreal, Maine and Atlantic Railway's operations director, Jean Demaître. Labrie and Aubé wanted to send another locomotive engineer to the scene, but the only locomotive engineer on staff was on vacation. They agreed to instead send Montreal, Maine and Atlantic Railway track foreman Jean-Noël Busque to ensure the fire was extinguished. He arrived at the scene at 12:34 a.m.

But Busque, as a track maintenance employee, had little knowledge of locomotives. He was unaware that turning off the engine had disabled the lead locomotive's independent air brake, the only remaining securement device on the train beside the handbrakes. Labrie, who was also a locomotive engineer, had been told that the locomotive had been shut down, but he apparently assumed that Harding had applied a sufficient number of handbrakes to keep the train from moving. He did not ask Harding how many handbrakes he'd applied before he left the train.

Labrie had called Harding at l'Eau Berge around midnight informing him of the fire. He told Harding the firefighters had put out the blaze and that Busque was on his way to the site.

"Is there someone there to take care of it? Do I need to go up there, start . . ." asked Harding. "Call me back."

"No, no, no," replied Labrie. "Go to bed."

Harding: "There's nothing to do, hey?"

Labrie: "There's nothing to do, we won't start up an engine now. For tomorrow morning. He's gonna start them up, the American is gonna start them up."

Labrie would have known that under mandatory rest requirements for engineers, Harding's returning to the train would mean that he would not be back on the job at the scheduled time to pilot the westbound train with empty tank cars the next morning — another costly delay.

At 12:30 a.m., Demaître called Labrie for an update, asking why the lead locomotive had been left running. He was informed that it had been left running to avoid having to perform an air brake test the next day. Busque and the remaining firefighter, Patrick Grégoire, confirmed to Labrie that the fire was out and the locomotive had been shut down. The men left the scene at 12:48 a.m.

At 12:58 a.m., an hour after the lead locomotive 5017 had been turned off, the air pressure in its air brake system leaked out to the point where the system, combined with the seven handbrakes, could no longer hold the train.[8]

Prime Minister Brian Mulroney with Deputy Prime Minister Eric Nielsen: the beginning of railway deregulation.

Bill Ackman, CEO of New York-based Pershing Square Capital Management hedge fund, with Hunter Harrison, his pick for President and CEO of CP.

Source: Fred Lum/*The Globe and Mail*

Irving refinery, Saint John NB, destination of the CP–Montreal, Maine and Atlantic train carrying Bakken shale oil from New Town, North Dakota via Lac-Mégantic.

Source: Alamy

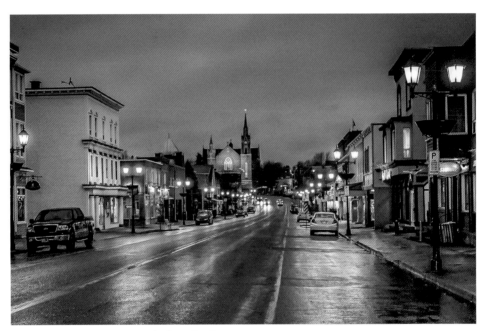

Downtown Lac-Mégantic: before the disaster.

Downtown Lac-Mégantic: after the disaster.

The inferno caused by the derailment.

Lac-Mégantic burning (smoldering).

Smoldering ruins of houses destroyed by the inferno.

Montreal, Maine and Atlantic lead locomotive 5017 that caught fire at Nantes on a hill 11 kilometres from Lac-Mégantic the night of July 5, 2013.

Prime Minister Stephen Harper and Industry Minister and MP for Lac-Mégantic-Érable, Christian Paradis, at a press conference following the disaster.

Lac-Mégantic Mayor Collette Roy-Laroche speaking to reporters in the disaster's aftermath.

Memorial for the victims.

Members of the Coalition des citoyens meeting with Transport Minister Marc Garneau.
From left to right: Gilles Fluet, Robert Bellefleur, Garneau, Gilbert Carette, and André
Blais.

Ed Burkhardt, owner of Montreal, Maine and Atlantic Railway, besieged by reporters near the site of the disaster.

Source: THE CANADIAN PRESS/Ryan Remiorz

Prime Minister Stephen Harper with Transport Minister Lisa Raitt, who replaced Denis Lebel shortly after the disaster.

Montreal, Maine and Atlantic Railway employees: Tom Harding, Jean Demaître and Richard Labrie, perp-walked into the courthouse in Lac-Mégantic to be criminally charged for the disaster.

Wendy Tadros, Transportation Safety Board chair and Don Ross, investigator-in-charge, at the news conference following the release of its Lac-Mégantic investigation report.

CHAPTER 8

Apocalypse[1]

The Musi-Café was a popular spot in the historic town centre of Lac-Mégantic, located on Frontenac Street just fifteen metres from the railway tracks. Boasting a richly diverse food menu and more than sixty different beers from around the world personally selected by its owner, Yannick Gagné, the bar was a magnet for tourists and residents alike. Among the lunchtime guests on Friday, July 5, was the federal industry minister, local Member of Parliament Christian Paradis, in town to announce a new youth employment program.

Around the time patrons were enjoying lunch on the terrace under a hot afternoon sun, the Montreal, Maine and Atlantic Railway train hauling seventy-two cars laden with Bakken crude oil was leaving Farnham, some two hundred kilometres away.

That evening, the Musi-Café was packed with people, many of them celebrating birthdays and family reunions. It was the final evening of a three-day residency by popular Quebec musicians Guy Bolduc and Yvon Ricard, who had been drawing large audiences. Best of friends, the two had begun their musical careers together in Lac-Mégantic twenty-five years before. The crowd was enthusiastic, calling out requests. The dance floor was packed.

At 11 p.m., as the Montreal, Maine and Atlantic Railway oil train pulled up at Nantes eleven kilometres away, the town centre was humming with activity. Throngs of people filled the sidewalks along Frontenac Street. Local residents, along with tourists in town from their lakeside cottages and campgrounds, chatted with friends and family, enjoying the warm, starry night. At midnight there were still some fifty people inside the Musi-Café and thirty on the terrace.

At 12:58 a.m., as the oil train began to roll, the crowds had thinned out. At the Musi-Café, the band had taken a break. Ricard's wife, who had joined him from Quebec City, had left for their hotel shortly before. Ricard stepped outside onto the terrace for a cigarette while Bolduc, a non-smoker, remained inside.

A few witnesses saw the ghostly train streaking across the countryside, gaining speed as it drew nearer to Lac-Mégantic. One of the firefighters who had attended the engine fire, Jean-Luc Montminy, was returning home when he came to a level crossing about six kilometres from Lac-Mégantic. The red lights were flashing. "I stopped my vehicle. Then I asked myself questions, because I did not hear a whistle, no engine," Montminy recalled. "I went a little further to have good visibility. I did not see anything, so I thought it's a mistake with the lights. I decided to cross. At that moment, the train appeared in front of my vehicle. It was travelling very fast. I assumed it was the same train we had been working on." He called 911.

A woman described the whooshing sound of the train as it blew past her house: not the usual slow chugging, and without the normal blast of its whistle at the nearby level crossing. As the train approached the outskirts of town, another woman, who was putting gas in her car at a service station, was shocked to see the train roar past. At this point, about three kilometres from the heart of town, the grade steepened and the train accelerated.

André Blais lived by the lake near the tracks, about a kilometre from the town centre. He heard a loud, rapid rat-a-tat-tat as the train roared past. The slope was steepest at this point. Seconds later, at 1:14 a.m., the driverless train derailed at a curve in front of the St. Agnès church in the heart of Lac-Mégantic. It had reached a speed of 105 kilometres per hour.

The five locomotives continued past the curve; the buffer car attached to the locomotives derailed first, and behind it sixty-three oil tank cars crashed, piled on top of each other. Most of them were punctured and more than fifty of them disgorged their incendiary contents. Almost immediately, said Blais, "the explosions began: first a series of small explosions, then two massive blasts and an orange mushroom cloud: the beginning of a long, apocalyptic night, a nightmare seared forever in our memories."

Gilles Fluet had left the Musi-Café a little earlier than usual and was walking home along Frontenac Street. He had just crossed the tracks when he saw the train hurtling toward him at high speed, then derail and explode. "The train missed me by four feet," he said. The heat from the explosion melted the nylon fibres of his shirt deep into his skin.

Yvon Rosa and his partner, Nathalie Guy, had decided before the last set to call it a night. They said goodbye to their musician friends Bolduc and Ricard, and were walking up Frontenac Street toward the tracks when they saw the train coming at "a crazy speed," Rosa remembers. "I was sure it wouldn't make the curve." He cried, "It's going to crash!" He saw the cars derail and the sparks fly, followed by explosions. "Run, run, run!" he yelled to Guy.

The couple hid in a lane between two buildings as a river of fire passed on either side. Seconds later, they bolted for the lake, jumping over fences and hedges. They didn't know what direction the fire would take as they raced for their condo by the lake, where they jumped into their boat to outrun the flames. "We were incredibly lucky . . . We lost many friends," says Rosa.

People on the terrace of the Musi-Café heard a rumbling sound, then another, louder this time. Then the train appeared. "It's going to derail!" someone yelled. The five locomotives roared past. There was a series of loud blasts, followed by the shrieking whistle of escaping gas, then the succession of fireballs and explosions.

A taxi whose driver was waiting for a fare in front of the bar screeched away from the curb. People ran for their lives toward the lake or the river. They felt unbearable heat and a tsunami of flames close on their heels, swallowing everything in its path. Windows shattered; electric boxes on telephone poles exploded.

Inside the Musi-Café, there was a first vibration, like an earthquake, then another, this time more violent. People froze, not realizing what was happening. The power failed. The bar went black, and then was illuminated by a blinding orange light outside.

Christian Lafontaine, who was at the back of the bar, reacted quickly. Grabbing his wife, Mélanie Guérard, he pulled her outside. "She just wanted to hide, everyone wanted to hide," Lafontaine recalled. There was no screaming, but with the orange light coming through the windows, many people mistakenly thought it was safer to stay inside the bar rather than go outside. They were the last to leave the Musi-Café alive.

At the front door, Lafontaine encountered his brother, Gaétan, who was going back in to get his wife, Joanie Turmel, who had gone to the washroom. Outside, Christian saw a wave of fire as wide as the street coming toward them. "When I saw the fire coming down the street, I knew it was oil," he said. "I just started running, racing south."

Behind them, tank cars began exploding as buildings crackled in the heat. They reached the south end of town and crossed the bridge over the Chaudière River, fearing downtown would turn to ash. Gaétan's body was found near his wife Joanie's at the back of the bar. "They were together, they found each other," Christian said. "That makes me feel better." The two had been childhood sweethearts.

Pascal Charest was talking to a friend at a taxi stand on Frontenac Street when the train derailed. His daughters, Bianka and Alyssa Charest Bégnoche, and their mother, Talitha Coumi Bégnoche, were asleep in their apartment near the Musi-Café.

He heard the rumble of the approaching train. When hydro lines began to collapse and a flash of light appeared, he knew something was terribly wrong, and that his children were in danger. He started running toward their apartment. A few metres from the door, he was stopped by a wall of flames. He circled around to try to reach them through the back door, but the flames there were even worse.

Musi-Café cook Bernard Trépanier was having a cigarette on the bar's terrace when he saw the train hurtling out of control and the cars wrenching off the tracks. He ran around to the Musi-Café's emergency exit. The heat was unbearable. He burned his arm trying to open the door. He could not help those trapped inside. He had to save himself. He ran back to the terrace, picked up his bike and fled. Once at a safe distance, he started banging on doors, warning people to get out.

Musi-Café waitress Karine Blanchette, who had finished her shift at 5 p.m. then performed in a local theatre production, had decided to return to her workplace for a drink with her colleagues. She wasn't able to find parking on Frontenac Street, so she decided to return home instead. In her rear-view mirror, she saw a ball of fire.

She pulled over and called her close friend and fellow server, Maude Verreault, who was working that night. No answer. But Maude called her back. She had been on break, having a cigarette on the terrace with her musician friend Ricard. They saw the train streak by, saw cars derail and heard the grinding sound of metal on metal, followed by explosions and a tsunami of flames rolling toward them. They ran for their lives.

Yannick Gagné, the Musi-Café owner, had gone home from the bar earlier than usual, at 12:30 a.m., to relieve the babysitter. He was followed shortly after by his wife. As they were getting ready to turn in for the night, Gagné felt the ground shake. Looking out the window, he saw the sky had turned brilliant orange. He thought a meteor had struck the town.

"One of my employees was calling," he said. "She was screaming, telling me that she was running away, that everything was on fire, it was chaos, the restaurant was gone, everything was gone, and people were still inside. I told her to calm down, that I'd go see." He left the house running, shirtless, toward the bar but was blocked by a wall of fire and crumpled tank cars.

Adrien Aubert was planning to go to the Musi-Café with a group of friends, but they'd decided to stay at his house, five minutes from the bar. For a moment, he thought he was hearing fireworks but then realized that was impossible; it was far too loud. He ran outside, reflexively grabbing his camera. The video he took was to be seen by millions of people around the world.

The audio recording captured Aubert breathing heavily as he moved along the perimeter of the fire: "*Oh, mon dieu, oh la la!* I have to back up. It's mind-blowing." He called his girlfriend, Karine, reporting: "I'm 200 metres from the town centre. The tank cars are exploding — I have never seen anything like it. Don't approach, Karine. It's crazy. The whole town is on fire."

Fire and black, billowing smoke filled his lens; the video captured sirens, flashing lights, firefighters, the constant roar and whistling of escaping gas and the dark contour of the nine tank cars that had not derailed, located dangerously close to the blaze. Then came a giant explosion.

"*Oh mon dieu, oh mon dieu,* oh my god, my god!" he gasped. "Don't worry about me, Karine. I'm being careful."

The experience of Rémi Tremblay, editor of the local weekly newspaper, *L'Écho de Frontenac,* was captured in a diaristic article he wrote entitled "La ville des âmes en peine" ("The town of souls in pain"). He wrote, in French:

> Awakened abruptly by my son Pierre in a panic. Quick, we have to evacuate. The town centre is on fire. On automatic pilot and in panic mode, woke up my partner, Marie-Douce, and the children, Felix and Maillée. We leave quickly. On the stairs, Pierre remembers his car keys are somewhere in the kitchen. In the dark, thank god, he finds them. Seconds of anguish: rapid departure. Time to join my daughter Anne-Marie on Laviolette Street, and we all head for Nantes.
>
> . . . No one knows what's happening, but the sky is on fire, a chain of explosions and the sound of whistling gas escaping from everywhere, the vomiting bowels of hell. The scene was like the end of the world.
>
> Yvon [Ricard] runs, a torrent of flames in hot pursuit. Bombs-on-rail overturn, pile one on top of the other,

empty and burn. Some outrun the flames, the heat intense on their backs. Another tries to get in his car. The tsunami of flames leaves him no chance.

Two kilometres away, staff at the local hospital saw the flash and heard the explosion; they knew something terrible had happened. The hospital went into "code orange" as staff quickly prepared for the expected onslaught of the injured. Staff from surrounding medical centres rushed in to help.

But the hospital remained eerily quiet. A Red Cross volunteer voiced the dawning realization: "You have to understand: there are no wounded. They're all dead." The local parish priest, Father Steve Lemay, recalled: "I went to the hospital to try to help with the wounded. We kept waiting, and the longer we waited, the more it became clear that there would be no injuries, only death."

Some residents risked their lives, knocking on doors to wake up their neighbours and helping them to flee. So too did the firefighters and Sûreté du Québec officers, who were on the scene within minutes of the blast.

Multiple explosions rocked the town, forming giant mushroom clouds as fiery oil poured through the downtown core, eviscerating buildings and flooding into the sewers, the lake, the river and the land. The sky above Lac-Mégantic, transformed by the light, could be seen from afar, like a strange sunrise surrounded by blackness. It was 1,650 degrees Celsius at the core of the blaze. The disaster zone was two times larger than that of the World Trade Center.

"EVERYTHING IS ON FIRE"

At 1:47 a.m., Tom Harding called the Farnham rail traffic controller, Richard Labrie, whose nickname was RJ. "Emergency; the town of Lac-Mégantic is on fire," Harding said. "Everything is on fire: from the church all the way down to the Metro, from the river all the way to the railway tracks. From what I can see, RJ, the boxcars have all burnt in the yard — the ties, everything. Whatever is in the yard, rolling stock, is now gone — completely.

"Flames, RJ, are 200 feet high. It's incredible; you can't believe it here.

From the river right to the station."

Harding thought the inferno had to have been caused by something like a natural gas pipeline. Definitely not his train. In the rapid evacuation, he was unable to find his American replacement engineer, Mark Samson, who was also staying at the hotel.

Shortly after 2 a.m., Daniel Aubé, the track supervisor, called Jean-Noël Busque who had gone to check the train an hour and a half earlier when it was still at Nantes asking him to head to Lac-Mégantic to see what was happening. Busque arrived on the scene, horrified by the magnitude of the destruction and unaware of its cause; Labrie had assured him the Montreal, Maine and Atlantic Railway train was still back at Nantes. Busque decided to return to Nantes.

At 2:10 a.m., Labrie called his boss, Jean Demaître. "What I want to know is if it's our train that ran down," said Labrie. "It's stressing the hell out of me." Demaître then asked him if Harding had secured his train. "Yes," replied Labrie. Demaître: "I fucking hope it's someone else's fault, not ours."

Fifteen minutes later, taxi dispatcher Clément Rancourt called Labrie to confirm that their train had run away, derailed and exploded in the town centre.

"It's burning like hell, man. There is no more downtown, Richard."

"*Calisse* . . . Oh no!" Labrie replied. Labrie then called Demaître again. "Put on your pants; the train rolled down."

"You're kidding me!" replied Demaître. "We're in deep shit, *tabarnac*, [Harding] didn't secure it properly."

At 3:29 a.m., Harding called Labrie again.

Labrie: "It's your train that rolled down."

Harding: "No!"

Labrie: "Yes sir."

Harding: "No RJ."

Labrie: "Yes sir. That's what I got. It was confirmed at 2:25."

Harding: "Oh, *tabarnac de tabarnac*! And it was secure, RJ, when I left. How in the fuck did that thing fucking roll down, RJ? I don't know."

Labrie: "How many brakes did you put on?"

Harding: "The units, the VB and the first car . . . seven brakes."

Labrie: "Apparently it rolled down. When it hit that fucking curve there it must have derailed."

The tank cars that were still intact posed an imminent hazard of even more explosions. Resident Guy Morin retrieved a railcar mover from the nearby Tafisa plant, where he worked. He and four other men were able to haul back five of the cars, but they could not re-enter the tracks with the mover to detach the remaining four cars.

Pascal Lafontaine, learning of their problem, brought a front-end loader from his family's construction business. But the loader did not have the necessary tool to deactivate the tank cars' air brakes.

Harding arrived on the scene wearing a firefighter's suit he had obtained from one of the firefighters. He unhooked and pulled the remaining cars to safety. The firefighters said he risked his life to do so.

Harding called Labrie one more time that night.

"I don't feel too good right now," Harding said.

"I understand. Me neither, I don't feel good," replied Labrie. "I can't believe the damage in downtown Mégantic. I can't imagine, maybe because I don't want to imagine. I guess it must be fucking hell."

"It is," replied Harding.

At dawn, an exhausted Harding took a taxi to make the two-hundred-kilometre trip back to Farnham. He slept most of the way home.

TOO POWERFUL TO FIGHT

More than one thousand firefighters from eighty municipalities in Quebec and six counties in Maine responded to the emergency call from the Lac-Mégantic fire department, with around 150 working on-site at any given time.

The heat was so intense that water from the hoses evaporated before it could reach the flames. Between that problem and the risk of further explosions, there was really nothing they could do on the night of the disaster to fight the fire. Their efforts focused on evacuating residents.

Burning oil had spread into the lake, setting several buildings, including the town marina, on fire. Flames also coursed through a four-foot-diameter storm pipe running from the train yard to the Chaudière River. The burning oil infiltrated sewers, and flames erupted from manholes, launching their covers into the air like flying saucers.

By morning of Saturday, July 6, a thousand people had been evacuated. The next morning, the municipality and the Red Cross set up a 250-bed shelter at the local high school, Polyvalente Montignac. While many evacuees had found shelter with family and friends, the waiting list for shelter was double that number. That afternoon, another thousand people, who lived downwind from the blast, were evacuated due to dangerous levels of toxic fumes.

On Tuesday, July 8, 1,200 people were allowed to return to their homes, but another six hundred, whose homes were closest to the epicentre, were still prohibited from returning. Two days later, almost all but those whose homes had been destroyed were allowed to return.

Four investigators from the Transportation Safety Board arrived on Saturday, as did a team from Sûreté du Québec, which immediately declared it a crime scene. Medical teams and grief counsellors provided treatment and support to the survivors and the victims' families. The Red Cross, Salvation Army, churches and other organizations were on-site providing food, clothing and shelter.

Municipal leaders like Mayor Colette Roy-Laroche — a grandmother and former primary school teacher — worked tirelessly, consoling families, receiving visitors, dealing with police and investigators and speaking to the media throng. Officials from Transport Canada, Environment Canada and the Quebec environment and health ministries were also there. In all, there were ten federal and twenty-three provincial ministries or agencies represented on the scene.

Late Saturday afternoon, firefighters announced that the blaze had been contained, but not extinguished. Since Transport Canada regulations did not require emergency response plans to be formulated in the event of a crude oil derailment, local firefighters were not equipped with the proper foam concentrate to put out a fire of this type. It took twenty-one hours for the foam to arrive from the Valero refinery in Lévis, 180 kilometres away.

Workers in the now-barricaded disaster zone were still using protective gear and breathing masks four days after the derailment, able to last for only fifteen-minute shifts due to heat exhaustion. The smouldering, heaped carcasses of tank cars created a landscape of desolation and ruin. The stench of fuel was overpowering.

It took almost three days for the fire to be completely extinguished. A sign was posted on the tracks near the crash site, which read: "You, the train from hell; do not come back here; you're not welcome."

A rainbow-hued slick covered the Chaudière River, drifting south toward the St. Lawrence. A company specializing in marine oil-spill response set up booms to contain the oil. Together with staff from Quebec's environment ministry, they worked day and night to plug pipes that were excreting oil into the river and lake. A team of Environment Canada specialists was also on site, advising first responders and evaluating the contamination of the lake and river. A boil-water advisory was issued, and municipalities downstream from the Chaudière River were warned to closely monitor their water.

Forensic experts from the Quebec coroner's office worked endlessly to identify victims' remains. By July 19, forty-seven people were confirmed dead, or missing and presumed dead. In some cases, identities were confirmed through DNA traces. For five victims, not even DNA was found.

Premier Pauline Marois arrived in town on Saturday. The next day, Prime Minister Harper toured the disaster site. Their governments pledged $60 million each to address the emergency and to rebuild the town.

As the world's media descended on the traumatized town, prodding with their microphones, residents exhibited extraordinary grace. Virtually no one in the town had been spared the shock and anguish of losing friends and loved ones.

When retired Transport Canada tank car specialist Jean-Pierre Gagnon learned of the tragedy, he said: "Well that's it; it's happened." He had been warning about such a disaster for years. He told *La Presse* that, given the inertia in the industry, he felt "there would have to be an accident with deaths for things to change. Sadly, I was right. When there are no deaths, we forget quickly."

BURKHARDT ARRIVES

On Wednesday, four days after the disaster, Montreal, Maine and Atlantic Railway owner Ed Burkhardt arrived in Lac-Mégantic. Burkhardt was clearly unprepared for a crisis of this magnitude and the anger that confronted him. He joked before arriving that he would need to wear a bulletproof vest, but had insisted that he didn't want a public-relations person to accompany him. The initial press statement was in English only.

At an impromptu press conference surrounded by a hostile crowd not far from the ashes of the Musi-Café, the tall, angular Burkhardt faced reporters questions. In a gravelly, nasal monotone he replied: "I'm absolutely devastated. I just don't know what to say."

But his nervous laugh seemed to belie his claim of empathy. His attempt to evade responsibility also didn't sit well. At first, he blamed the firefighters for turning off the lead locomotive while the train was in Nantes. He then shifted blame to Harding for not applying enough handbrakes, adding that Harding had been suspended without pay.

His tone-deafness was reflected in his answer to a reporter inquiring about his net worth. Burkhardt smirked: "A whole lot less than yesterday." One person in the crowd interviewed by reporters asked: "How can he sleep at night? I can't sleep."

Burkhardt wasn't given access to the disaster site. He also claimed he was not given an audience with the mayor. The mayor retorted that it was Burkhardt who cancelled the meeting.

Burkhardt's brief appearance in Lac-Mégantic was a public-relations disaster. CNN labelled him "the most despised person in Canada." In an interview with Wolf Blitzer, he admitted: "People misunderstood me. I didn't present my case very well."

A few days later, taking refuge in four layers of subsidiary corporate entities and the veil of limited liability, Burkhardt told *Maclean's* that the corporate form of Montreal, Maine and Atlantic Railway was merely an instrument controlled by human beings: "a bank account in a lockbox at the post office. It doesn't do things. People do things."

It was clear what people he was referring to. Again pointing the finger at Harding, Burkhardt continued to deny his own responsibility. No major policy, investment or operational decision was made without his consent. Confronted outside his home by a Radio-Canada journalist holding out a picture of the youngest victim of the disaster, four-year-old Alyssa Charest Bégnoche, Burkhardt quivered, "I'm very, very upset about this. What more can I say? I'm devastated by this whole thing."

CHAPTER 9

Aftermath

When Prime Minister Harper visited Lac-Mégantic on Sunday, the day after the disaster, he compared the site to a war zone. Harper promised federal financial support for the community's reconstruction. He vowed that the disaster would be fully investigated by the Transportation Safety Board and the police and promised to draw lessons from their findings: "We will conduct a very complete investigation and we will act on the recommendations."

The following Tuesday, Transport Minister Denis Lebel came to the still-smouldering town. Speaking to reporters and the public, Lebel was defensive about the safety records of both the government and the rail freight industry. He insisted that the DOT-111 tank cars were suitable for carrying crude and denied the fact that his government had made cuts to the rail safety budget. At a time that called for empathy with victims' families and solidarity with the community, Lebel's performance left a bad taste.

A week later, Lebel was out as transport minister, and Lisa Raitt was in. He would not have to respond to uncomfortable questions from parliamentarians and journalists, neatly ducking ministerial responsibility.

But Lebel's ineptness before the microphones may have contributed to his downfall. With the public's confidence in the government's ability to protect their safety at a low point, Harper, at minimum, needed a better communicator. On this front, Raitt, despite her French-language limitations, was considerably more qualified to stickhandle her government through the crisis. She was used to responding to flak as former CEO of the Toronto Port Authority, a federal body that had a history of thwarting the government of Toronto, most famously by successfully engineering an airport expansion on the formerly idyllic Toronto Islands.

The crisis, however, was not just political. Lac-Mégantic sent shudders of panic through Transport Canada. A catastrophe of this magnitude had only come up on the radar of a few Cassandras, including Jean-Pierre Gagnon. Four days after the crash, Transport Canada officials sent an urgent memo to Montreal, Maine and Atlantic Railway demanding that it add a new communication protocol to ensure rail traffic controllers ask locomotive engineers how many handbrakes they have applied. This was a first sign of Transport Canada's acknowledgement that its less-than-adequate oversight bore some of the responsibility for what went wrong.

Transport Canada was worried that its failure to make one-person trains conditional on this rule *before* the disaster would become an issue in the Transportation Safety Board investigation that was already under way. Alain Richer, an inspector from the Quebec office, was on-site from the beginning as Transport Canada's official observer.

Richer briefed the minister on developments; the department also prepared a briefing document for the minister. It noted that practices allowed under the current regulatory framework "may have contributed to the chain of events that led to the incident, and magnified its consequences." Among those mentioned were allowing locomotives to be left unlocked and unattended on a main track, the use of single-person crews and carrying dangerous goods in tank cars.

The briefing recommended that Transport Canada take the unusual step of issuing a emergency directive that no locomotive hauling dangerous goods be left unattended on a main track and that no locomotive hauling dangerous goods be operated with a crew of less than two.

From the start, Transport Canada officials were fairly certain that, with the directive, they had identified contributing factors to the disaster. The briefing note also recommended that companies submit their operating instructions on brake securement to Transport Canada.

The briefing argued that getting a jump on the Transportation Safety Board findings would demonstrate leadership. But it also cautioned that the directive could give rise to questions as to why these practices had been allowed in the first place. This sensitive matter was addressed in talking points. Among them: Transport Canada was "now explicitly aware of certain industry practices which could have a risk of diminishing safety on Canada's railways."

On July 19, the Transportation Safety Board issued a recommendation to Transport Canada that trains carrying dangerous goods not be left unattended on a main track, and that they be properly secured. The Transportation Safety Board recommendations, as well as those from Transport Canada officials, were all included in an emergency directive on July 23, 2013.

In the immediate aftermath of the tragedy, the responses of federal government and the railway industry followed a predictable pattern observed in previous catastrophes, such as the Ocean Ranger sinking and the Westray Mine explosion. There were expressions of sympathy for the families and the community; commitments to get to the bottom of what happened; and company statements that they were reviewing their safety procedures, public safety being their highest priority.

But no blame was accepted. It was directed elsewhere, usually at the easiest and most vulnerable target, the workers closest to the event.

By December 2013, Harper was telling reporters that, although an investigation was still under way, "I think that the facts that we do know indicate pretty clearly that rules were not abided by."[1] Raitt and other government leaders repeated the same slogan: "The government puts the rules in place; the rules were not followed." Harper was not inclined to probe deeply into underlying causes. It was the sort of thing he equated with "committing sociology."

After blaming firefighters and Harding for the disaster, Burkhardt turned his sights on the shipper for misclassifying the oil's volatility. Yet Burkhardt was the very personification of Montreal, Maine and Atlantic Railway; no major decision regarding company policy, operations or investments was made without his stamp on it. He denied that single-person train operation was a cause of the tragedy, and told an American reporter that they were a financial necessity in a business-unfriendly state like Maine.

CP CEO Hunter Harrison — whose company had contracted with Irving and subcontracted with Montreal, Maine and Atlantic Railway — also blamed Harding for not setting enough handbrakes. But he did not stop there. He cast blame on tank-car owners for stonewalling efforts to build safer cars. Others to blame, in Harrison's view, included oil companies and Transport Canada. There was a lot of blame to go around, yet Harrison also scolded the Conservative government for overreacting to Lac-Mégantic.

Railway Association of Canada president Michael Bourque assured the public of his industry's commitment to learning from the disaster. Initially, the association denied that it had proposed scrubbing a rule requiring human inspection of tank cars carrying dangerous goods. Two days after the tragedy, the association withdrew its request. And Bourque was silent on the association's pressuring the government to let Montreal, Maine and Atlantic Railway run one-person oil trains.

While publicly denying responsibility for the disaster, the industry, behind closed doors, was urging the government not to impose any new regulations. In the three months following the disaster, the Railway Association lobbied senior officials and politicians sixteen times. This included nine contacts with the transport minister's office, two of them with the minister herself. This volume of lobbying activity exceeded that of any other three-month interval between 2010 and 2015.[2] Indeed, in one of her first actions as minister, Raitt met with lobbyists from CN and CP. What was discussed at those meetings has never been revealed, despite multiple requests for briefing notes under access to information law.

A VOLATILE DEBATE

In September, two months after the disaster, Transportation Safety Board investigators issued a safety advisory letter revealing that the crude oil on the Lac-Mégantic train was more volatile (PG II, equivalent to gasoline) than indicated by its classification documents, which described it as low-volatility PG III. But at a press conference, investigators said that even if the cargo had been properly classified, it would still have been allowed in the standard DOT-111 tank cars. They also noted that the importer, Irving Oil, had the ultimate responsibility to ensure the product was properly classified.

In response, Transport Canada issued a directive requiring that oil be tested prior to shipment into Canada to confirm it was less volatile than PG I, and in the interim that it be assigned the highest volatility level, namely PG I. North Dakota shippers told the *Globe and Mail* that, for speed's sake, they simply labelled outbound crude PG I without stopping to test it. In other words, shippers had no better idea of the volatility of their product than before the disaster.[3]

The Harper government's fall Throne Speech promised to introduce measures to improve rail safety and legislation to ensure companies had sufficient insurance to cover Lac-Mégantic–magnitude accidents. However, its simultaneous commitment to freeze program spending and hiring seemed to contradict the rail-safety promise.

In another sign of business as usual, the Canadian and American governments announced the following year their intention to harmonize rulemaking under the bilateral Regulatory Cooperation Council. The plan, according to a Harper government press release, would help "reduce the burden on business, thereby boosting North American trade and competitiveness."[4]

In November, Transport Minister Raitt asked the House of Commons transport committee to investigate the transportation of dangerous goods and the role of the safety management system regime across all modes of transportation. Though they can be a valuable source of testimony, such parliamentary committee investigations are subject to tight political control. The minister dismissed calls for an independent judicial inquiry, which, in contrast, could not be controlled.

In December 2013, Transport Canada approved changes to the Canadian Rail Operating Rules, entrenching the post–Lac-Mégantic emergency directive banning single-person crews for freight trains carrying dangerous goods.

The change was made over the objections of the rail lobby. But where the Railway Association of Canada was unsuccessful in trying to roll back this directive, it had more luck with the directive requiring that trains carrying dangerous goods not be left unattended on a main track. The Railway Association instead proposed a set of securement rules, which would allow trains carrying dangerous goods to be left unattended for two hours with only the air brakes applied. Despite opposition both internally and externally, Transport Canada acceded, reversing the directive at the beginning of 2014.

As late as mid-January 2014, Raitt was denying that conventional DOT-111 tank cars were a major cause for concern, even though several oil trains had derailed and spilled since Lac-Mégantic. "These cars are safe. They can transport the goods and they do so safely 99.997 per cent of the time," she said, repeating the industry statistic.[5] "What we want to do is get it better and do it right in consultation with all parties: the shippers, the rail companies and of course our cousins in the United States."

Ten days later, in an unprecedented joint move, the Canadian and American transportation safety boards issued a recommendation calling for the rapid phase-out of DOT-111 cars.

According to a former insider, the idea of a phase-out was opposed by the Harper government and senior Transport Canada officials. But Transportation Safety Board chair Wendy Tadros had pushed for it, supporting the outreach her staff had made to their American counterparts, even knowing it would likely mean that Harper would not reappoint her to another four-year term as chair.

The manoeuvre worked. The Federal Railroad Administration let it be known privately that it would take the lead on the DOT-111 phase-out if Canada failed to do so. The optics of following an American lead would have been bad for Ottawa.

Three months later, in April 2014, Tadros won the day, as Raitt issued a directive that transportation of crude oil in DOT-111 cars end by May 2017. Raitt also ordered the immediate elimination of five thousand of the most vulnerable DOT-111 cars. Soon after, the two regulators began formal consultations on a strengthened tank car design.

Also in April, Transport Canada implemented several additional measures. It committed to bringing in enhanced testing protocols for crude oil, as well as increased inspections, from the wellhead through to refinery, to verify the accuracy of dangerous-goods classifications. It ordered companies to provide updated risk assessments for each "key route" and to have measures in place to address these risks. However, they were protected under commercial confidentiality provisions and thus not accessible to the public.

Key routes were defined as those transporting ten thousand or more cars of dangerous goods annually. Thus the likes of Montreal, Maine and Atlantic Railway would not be covered, despite a Transportation Safety Board recommendation to lower the threshold.

Transport Canada also limited the speed of key-route trains carrying crude to fifty miles per hour, and forty miles per hour within urban areas. Though derailments had occurred at lower speeds than these mandated limits, the industry strongly resisted any further lowering of speeds.

Transport Canada also ordered railways to inform municipalities about dangerous goods passing through their communities, though not in real time. They were required to provide annual reports on the type and volume of dangerous goods carried, broken down by quarter. Municipalities, meanwhile, were obliged to sign legal commitments that they would not make this information public.

The new suite of measures also required railways carrying crude oil to prepare emergency-response assistance plans for each route. It specified that these plans should address the emergency-response capability of local fire departments and municipalities, and consult with the Federation of

Canadian Municipalities. But here again, the public was not let into the picture. Companies were not required to make their emergency-response assistance plans public, lest commercial confidentiality be breached.

The minister also announced the creation of an emergency-response task force, bringing together municipalities, first responders, railways and shippers.

It all sounded good on paper. But, as American rail-safety expert Fred Millar told an oil-train conference, "while emergency response is a natural reaction, it is in fact a distraction from what we have to do . . . We should not pretend that there is anything that one can do about a major crude-oil fire."

According to the US Department of Transport, there's no pretending even with a relatively minor fire. The department's Emergency Response Handbook gives this directive: "If only one crude oil or ethanol car is on fire, evacuate a half-mile and let the fires burn."

Lac-Mégantic demonstrated the effect of a high-magnitude accident in a small population centre. As horrific as that was, imagine, Millar said, the consequences of a hundred-car oil train derailment and fire in a major population centre. The first priority, according to Millar, should be prevention. But if one should occur, the most pressing priority is evacuation of people from the disaster zone.

The Transportation Safety Board had, a few months earlier, recommended that Transport Canada require that railways create alternative routes for transporting dangerous goods through densely populated or vulnerable areas. Transport Canada paid little heed to the recommendation, and the industry viewed it as unrealistic, given the linear nature of the country. As mentioned in Chapter 2, both major railways had torn up, without objection from Transport Canada, their Ottawa Valley lines, which *did* circumvent densely populated areas. Nor did the railways consider interchange agreements with other companies that might have offered safer routes.

A FIX FOR FATIGUE
From the time it came into force, back in the early days of the neoliberal

era in 1988, the *Railway Safety Act* reflected the power of the rail industry to both draft its own operating rules and to block, delay and dilute government regulations. New regulations implementing the 2013 amendments to the *Act* finally came into effect in March 2014. They gave Transport Canada new powers to suspend a company's licence — its railway operating certificate — or shut down a company entirely for violations of the *Act*, without having to resort to court action.

However, Transport Canada had diluted this new provision under pressure from the industry, insisting to companies that they could obtain their certificates with minimal red tape, a Harper government priority. A company had to submit a risk assessment. But the company simply had to *attest* that it met the "highest level of safety." Its risk assessment did not have to be submitted to Transport Canada. The message contained in the *Canada Gazette*, which publicizes new regulations, confirmed that industry pushback had successfully extracted its teeth: "Transport Canada would only cancel or suspend the railway operating certificate in extreme cases where there is company-wide or chronic non-compliance, or where their operation poses a serious risk to safe railway operations."[6] It raised the question: If these regulations had been in place a year earlier, would Transport Canada have shut down Montreal, Maine and Atlantic Railway?

The power of the railways also reflected efforts to bring in new regulations designed to manage crew fatigue. CBC reporters John Nicol and Dave Seglins obtained copies of draft minutes of a meeting between Transport Canada and the industry, whose atmosphere one participant described as heated.[7] The rail representatives challenged Transport Canada's research report, which Railway Association executive Kevin McKinnon described "as being written by someone who wants to shut the railways down at night."

The report found high levels of exhaustion among freight train operators. Workers were routinely awake for seventeen to nineteen hours, which is equivalent to being inebriated. (Montreal, Maine and Atlantic Railway engineer Tom Harding had been awake for over seventeen hours by the time he left the train, which the Transportation Safety

Board report determined impeded his judgment regarding the problem with the smoking locomotive.) The report proposed new limits on shift lengths — limits already in place in the US.

Clinton Marquardt, a fatigue specialist who worked on the Transportation Safety Board's Lac-Mégantic investigation, told the CBC that "enough is enough." It was high time to force rail companies to put their employees' biological need for sleep ahead of profits. A study by the National Sleep Foundation in the US also supported this view, concluding that working conditions meant that many transportation workers were not getting enough sleep. Nevertheless, fatigue management regulations remained ineffectual.

Transport Canada imposed an unprecedented order on CP in 2014, demanding the company change its fatigue management practices in British Columbia, which posed "an immediate threat to safe railway operations." CP pushed back. Vice-president Keith Creel urged that Transport Canada move past "emotional and deceptive rhetoric into the arena of fact."

All told, the flurry of government activity in the year following the Lac-Mégantic disaster sought to demonstrate that important lessons were learned and corrective action was being taken, that Ottawa was reaffirming its obligation to protect Canadian citizens, whose confidence had been shattered by Lac-Mégantic. Meanwhile, the Transportation Safety Board team was continuing its investigation into the causes of the tragedy. And it was reverberating south of the border as well.

STATESIDE ALARMS

Lac-Mégantic had raised alarms with US regulators. As in Canada, oil-by-rail traffic — most of it Bakken oil — had skyrocketed between 2009 and 2013. A series of major oil-train derailments and explosions followed in the year after Lac-Mégantic: at Aliceville, Alabama, in November 2013; a month later in Casselton, North Dakota; at Lynchburg, Virginia, in April 2014; and at the aptly named Mount Carbon, West Virginia, in February 2015. While none caused the devastation of Lac-Mégantic, there were several close calls that necessitated large-scale evacuations. The National Transportation Safety Board warned that major safety improvements were urgently needed.

The Federal Railroad Administration had also been concerned that the length and weight of oil trains was putting too much stress on tracks. The Associated Press had reported that efforts to improve safety via rail-wear regulations limiting train length and weight had been blocked by the industry back in 2013 in favour of voluntary guidelines.

In September 2013, the Department of Transportation called an emergency meeting of its Railroad Safety Advisory Committee to discuss ways of preventing a Lac-Mégantic in the US. Transport Canada's director general of rail safety, Luc Bourdon, provided a briefing.

A month earlier, in August, the Federal Railroad Administration and the Pipeline and Hazardous Materials Safety Administration had initiated Operation Classification, a series of unannounced inspections to verify the classification and volatility of Bakken oil. These "Bakken blitzes" inspected wellheads, loading terminals and other locations along the crude oil transportation chain.

Six months into the investigation, confirming the Transportation Safety Board finding in Canada, the administration issued an alert: Bakken oil could be more volatile than traditional crude. The following March, the Department of Transportation issued an emergency order requiring shippers to test Bakken oil and to treat it as highly volatile.

The Federal Railroad Administration investigation's final report on Operation Classification confirmed that Bakken crude had a higher gas content, a lower flashpoint, a lower boiling point and higher vapour pressure than other crude oils. Its characteristics were predominantly consistent with PG I — the highest volatility classification.

The US petroleum industry ramped up its deny-and-delay operation, maintaining that Bakken's high volatility was a myth. Contrary to assessments by safety investigators, regulators and independent experts, a brief by the American Fuel & Petrochemical Manufacturers made the disingenuous argument that carrying Bakken oil in DOT-111 cars was safe, *provided railroads keep the cars on the tracks.*

Investigative reporters Marcus Stern and Sebastian Jones provide fascinating insight into the power of industry and the rulemaking process in an article for *InsideClimate News.*[8] They reported that in January

2014, a hazardous materials working group was convened by the Federal Railroad Administration. In attendance were staff members, representatives from the American Petroleum Institute, the Association of American Railroads, companies and unions.

Safety proposals put forward by administration staff were vetoed. At one point, the head of the hazardous materials division argued for better communication between shippers and railways to ensure, for example, that aging bridges were able to handle the load. A lawyer representing the Association of American Railroads denied there was a problem, and the recommendation was shelved.

In another exchange, Cynthia Hilton, vice-president of the Institute of Makers of Explosives, said she thought the point of the meeting was to produce guidance for the industry, not requirements. "And now I'm reading that the shipper must develop and adhere to a sampling and testing program. That doesn't sound like a guidance document," she complained.

"You're right, and I agree," the hazardous materials director assured Hilton. "This is of course open for editing, ideas and suggestions. I circled the word 'must'; 'should' is probably a little more appropriate."

In April 2014, the Federal Railroad Administration indicated it would proceed with a rule establishing minimum crew size for most freight and passenger rail, including trains carrying crude oil. The railways immediately opposed it, demanding that the administration withdraw the proposal. Edward Hamberger, the Association of American Railroads' president and CEO, described it as "a textbook example of unnecessary regulation." "With no data showing that one-person operations compromise safety, there is no basis — other than anecdotal storytelling — for enacting a general prohibition on crew size reductions."

The same pattern was playing out in the US as in Canada. Regulatory capture, no longer in the shadows, was making its power visible.

CHAPTER 10

The Investigation That Lost Heart

An initial four-person investigative team arrived on a scene of chaos in Lac-Mégantic on the morning of July 6, 2013. They encountered the results of a rail accident of a magnitude never anticipated, and for which the agency had never planned.

The team leader was Don Ross, a well-respected veteran investigator from the Atlantic region. The team's numbers rose quickly, peaking at thirty. Rail investigators made up half of the team, with the rest consisting of support and communications personnel, an industrial psychologist and a dangerous goods expert from America. Transportation Safety Board staff members were brought in from Transportation Safety Board offices across the country.

The Sûreté du Québec had cordoned off the disaster zone, declaring it a crime scene under its exclusive control. This caused some tension at first, but an agreement was quickly reached that recognized the Transportation Safety Board's role as an independent federal agency with full access to the site.

The scale of the disaster presented the team with a variety of logistical challenges, including access to food, water and electronic communications.

The lack of accommodation forced the majority of team members to drive for up to two hours to and from the site every day. The return trip in particular was daunting after long, exhausting days.

And there were delays. The team had to wait for almost two days until the fire burned out. Then came a work interruption by heavy machinery operators concerned about whether they would be paid.

The team was on-site for twenty-seven days, after which members relocated to the Transportation Safety Board lab at Ottawa International Airport. The goal was to complete the investigation within the one-year time frame prescribed by Transportation Safety Board chair Wendy Tadros. In all, fifty people worked on the investigation, including experts brought in to examine specific aspects of the crash. Investigators travelled to several US locations, including North Dakota.

The Transportation Safety Board report was released, in Lac-Mégantic itself, on August 19, 2014, eleven months after the tragedy.

At the press conference — her last public act as chair — Tadros issued a withering condemnation of Transport Canada for allowing Montreal, Maine and Atlantic Railway's repeated safety violations to go unchecked or unpunished. "Who was the guardian of public safety? That's the role of government . . . And yet this booming industry — where unit trains were shipping more and more oil across Canada, and across the border — ran largely *un*checked."[1]

It was blunt language. But curiously, Tadros's hard-headed take had not informed the report she was releasing that day.[2] The dead horse of Montreal, Maine and Atlantic Railway got a good flogging, but the very actor in the room that made Montreal, Maine and Atlantic Railway possible, Transport Canada, got a slap on the wrist.

In that gulf lies the tale of an investigation whose conclusions went from illuminating to obscuring, that went from pursuing the public interest to covering the government and industry's hindquarters. The Transportation Safety Board's final report on Lac-Mégantic, by succumbing to political and industry pressure, betrayed its commitment to independence in determining the disaster's causes, thereby foregoing the opportunity to provide lessons critical to making the public safer.

THE ERASURE OF A CAUSE

As the report's findings went through revisions, its original edge was dulled. Most crucially, blame squarely placed on Transport Canada for allowing Montreal, Maine and Atlantic Railway to operate one-person oil trains was erased.

Each version of the report distinguished between two levels of factors behind the crash. The more direct type was characterized as "causes and contributing factors." The less direct type was called "risk factors."

The original report, dated April 1, 2014, was written by the investigators themselves. It listed twenty-seven causes and contributing factors to the disaster. No less than six flowed from Transport Canada's decision to allow Montreal, Maine and Atlantic Railway to operate one-person trains:

- Transport Canada approved the 2008 Railway Association rewrite of the Canadian Rail Operating Rules to allow solo trains without ensuring an equivalent level of safety compared to two-person crews.

- Montreal, Maine and Atlantic Railway's poor regulatory compliance, poor equipment and track condition, non-adherence to operating procedures and weak safety culture, all reflecting deficient oversight by Transport Canada, were not conducive to safe implementation of single-person crews.

- Although the shift to single-person crews was a significant operational change requiring risk assessment, Transport Canada did not provide adequate oversight of Montreal, Maine and Atlantic Railway to ensure risks were addressed.

- Training was insufficient to ensure that the lone engineer understood and applied rules and instructions correctly, another broken commitment by the company that was not caught by Transport Canada.

- The absence of a second crew member removed a key safety defence — and Transport Canada did not require the imposition of backup safety defences that would have ensured correct securement and allowed for consultation on the excessive smoke problem on locomotive 5017.

- There were no procedures for the locomotive engineer to confirm with the rail traffic controller the number of handbrakes applied in absence of a second person on site to confirm brake securement: a failure that was only rectified by Transport Canada after the damage had been done.

Two more causes were attributed to Transport Canada headquarters: It inadequately monitored its regional offices, failing to ensure effective oversight and risk management of short-line railways; and its inspections and safety management system audits were defective — infrequent, of limited scope and lacking follow-up.

A second version of the report, dated April 14, deleted all mention of one-person trains in the causes category.

A third version of the report, dated April 30, 2014, reinstated a single cause relating to one-person trains. It referred to the absence of compensatory measures regarding securement and included discussion of the engine fire problem.

However, the final version of the report, released on August 14, 2014, re-erased that one reinstated cause. The issue of one-person train operation was shifted to a vaguely worded statement in the risk category, out of the spotlight.

This whitewashing successfully diverted the media, whose stories on the report repeatedly referred to the eighteen causes, ignoring the risk factors, where the one-person issue had been shunted.

HOW DID THIS LAPSE COME ABOUT?

The Transportation Safety Board's mandate notes that "to instill confidence in the public regarding the transportation accident investigation process, it is essential that an investigating agency be independent and free from any conflicts of interest when investigating accidents, identifying safety deficiencies and making safety recommendations. As such, the Transportation Safety Board is an independent agency, separate from other government agencies and departments, that reports to Parliament through the president of the Privy Council and the minister of democratic institutions."

But far from being independent, on the Lac-Mégantic file the Transportation Safety Board bent to the wishes of the rail industry, Transport Canada and ultimately Prime Minister Harper. Partly this occurred out of deference, the board members being term political appointees unlike their predecessors. And partly it was the result of direct input from the apex of power on the final report. "The Prime Minister's Office's hands were all over it," according to one source — and those of the industry the Transportation Safety Board was supposed to be probing.

The interim version of the report, dated April 14, shows revisions made by Transportation Safety Board member Kathy Fox, in consultation with other members. (Harper would soon appoint Fox to succeed Tadros.) Raitt's office was receiving regular briefings about the investigation and was almost certainly aware of this report. Given the all-controlling nature of the prime minister, the Prime Minister's Office was also being briefed.

The railways were no doubt also aware of the original version as well as subsequent drafts of the report's conclusions, and were pushing hard to excise the one-person crew causes.

Both Transport Canada and the railways, according to a former insider, reacted fiercely when they saw the draft. Some board members were adamantly opposed to singling out one-person operations.

According to several sources, the Transportation Safety Board had become more actively involved in recent years, in contrast to what had traditionally been a hands-off approach with respect to investigation team conclusions. And Transportation Safety Board reports do not allow for minority reports on controversial issues. In the end, Tadros brokered the best consensus she could.

The erasure of one-person trains as a cause was deeply puzzling to expert observers. After all, single-person crews were deemed by the Transportation Safety Board to be a causal factor in other accidents, notably the 1996 Quebec North Shore and Labrador Railway accident. A 2009 Transportation Safety Board report had also warned against one-person crews: "When only one crew member is left to complete train securement tasks at the end of a work shift, the risk for runaway equipment is increased because there is no opportunity for other crew members to identify and correct any errors."[3] Said Steve Callaghan, who had an intimate knowledge of both incidents, "Transport Canada dropped the ball on single-person train operations, and the Transportation Safety Board missed the point entirely in their public report on the Mégantic tragedy."[4]

Although the Transportation Safety Board had the legal authority to convene public hearings, that option was foreclosed; it would have embarrassed the government. Raitt dismissed the idea of a judicial inquiry.

FUDGE FACTOR

The Lac-Mégantic report was Wendy Tadros's final act as Transportation Safety Board chair. She stepped down the day after its release, to be replaced by Kathy Fox. In an interview with Fox shortly after she assumed office, *Enquête* journalist Sylvie Fournier asked her why single-person train operation was not considered a cause of the crash. Fox replied, "We were not able to conclude if yes or no it would have changed the situation to have had a second crew member. We can't engage in speculation if we don't have a firm conclusion." This was curious, since the Transportation Safety Board traditionally made conclusions based on the balance of probabilities, according to a former insider.

Furthermore, Fox said there was evidence that a single-person crew was actually safer because he or she would not be distracted by a second crew member. This was the same rationale provided by Burkhardt. It also contradicted findings of earlier Transportation Safety Board investigations. When asked by Fournier whether any scientific studies corroborated her judgment, Fox replied in the affirmative and promised to provide this evidence. But she never did.

In fact, the scientific evidence confirmed the opposite assessment. A 2012 US Federal Railroad Administration report confirmed the importance of having at least two crew members on trains.[5] The report concluded that conductors and locomotive engineers work together as a unit to monitor the operating environment outside the locomotive cab, to plan, to solve problems and to identify and mitigate risk. But the conductor is also trained to supervise train operation for efficiency and safety. His or her role is to understand the impact of various factors (such as limitations imposed by train length and weight) on safe operation. The report also found that operating on a steep grade could significantly add to the complexity of the conductor's duties and thus to cognitive demands.

Speaking at an October 2015 conference, senior Transportation Safety Board staff member Don Mustard, who worked on the Lac-Mégantic investigation, contradicted his boss: "When you have an unexpected circumstance happening, then it really helps to have someone else to bounce your ideas against to try and figure things out," said Mustard. "For instance, with train securement, it's a lot easier to have one guy throwing the handbrakes and another guy holding the train with the equipment and testing to see that they're working."[6]

Common sense, it would seem.

Transport Minister Raitt responded to the Transportation Safety Board report, which she described as the last word on the cause of the tragedy, by repeating what had become her standard talking points: "We need to remember that in terms of safety, the government puts the rules in place. The companies are expected to follow the rules. The company did not follow the rules." Her remarks contrasted starkly with those of the Transportation Safety Board chair, Wendy Tadros, who stressed that employee responsibility was the last line of defence in railway safety; it was not a substitute for policy direction, management supervision and government oversight.

As for ministerial responsibility, both Raitt and her predecessor, Lebel, had an out. The Canadian Guidelines for Ministers written by Harper's Privy Council had been changed several years earlier, as described in Chapter 5.

The politicians were off the hook.

CHAPTER 11

Still Spilling

The Lac-Mégantic disaster jolted regulators in both Canada and the United States, setting in train a variety of measures. However modest, they nonetheless triggered battles, with industry doing its best to ignore, block, delay and dilute government actions.

In January 2015, six months after the Transportation Safety Board released its Lac-Mégantic report, the Conservative government introduced the *Safe and Accountable Rail Act*, amending the *Railway Safety Act*. Speaking in the House of Commons on behalf of the bill, Transport Minister Raitt stated: "We have learned the lessons inherent in past tragedies, and our commitment to safety is absolute . . . the safety and the security of Canadians remain the top priority of Transport Canada."

The *Act* bolstered the enforcement powers of both rail safety inspectors and the minister. Inspectors were given more authority to mitigate situations that reached the threat level. The minister could order companies to get their safety management systems up to scratch.

The *Act*'s main purpose, however, was to ensure that industry had enough insurance to cover future accidents, so government would be spared the tab. The *Act* set new liability insurance minimums for companies carrying crude oil and other dangerous goods. Depending on the type and volume of the goods transported, the new minimum coverage ranged from $25 million to $1 billion. It was a mild measure since CN and CP customarily carried more than $1 billion worth of liability insurance.

The *Act* also established a new fund, financed by a levy of $1.65 per tonne on shippers of crude oil, to cover liability costs in excess of companies' insurance. Transport Canada estimated that the levy would raise about $17 million per year and would take fifteen years to reach its $250-million target.

Would this suffice to cover a Lac-Mégantic–magnitude disaster? The methodology used to arrive at these numbers was not made public. Nor did the figures appear to cover environmental costs. The Lac-Mégantic disaster is estimated to have cost $1 billion, paid for mostly by governments. The company that replaced Montreal, Maine and Atlantic Railway, Central Maine & Quebec Railway, was required to have only $75 million in liability insurance.

A US Pipeline and Hazardous Materials Safety Administration report on the expected impact of trains carrying what it termed "high-hazard" flammable liquids estimated that over a twenty-year period, the US would experience ten additional "high-consequence" safety events, "nine of which would have environmental damages, and injury and fatality costs exceeding $1.15 billion [US]. The tenth would have environmental damages, injury and fatality costs exceeding $5.75 billion [US]." The Canadian government has not revealed whether it has produced a similar worst-case disaster scenario.

The Federation of Canadian Municipalities continued to be concerned about the level of transparency surrounding dangerous-goods trains running through their communities. Firefighters were still concerned about not getting real-time disclosure. Toronto City Council wrote to the transport minister, asking that trains carrying dangerous goods be rerouted around the city. A Toronto citizens group, Safe Rail Communities, filed an access to information request to obtain railway companies' route planning, risk assessments and emergency response plans. The entire document the group received was "redacted" — blacked out — on the grounds of commercial confidentiality.

TWO MORE DERAILMENTS

Shortly after the *Safe and Accountable Rail Act* was introduced, in February and March 2015, two CN derailments near Gogama in northern Ontario shattered the conventional wisdom that Alberta bitumen was safer than Bakken crude. The trains, carrying diluted bitumen in CPC-1232 tank cars, spilled a combined four million litres, which exploded and burned for days. This particular tank car model, in the words of a US National Transportation Board member, is "a slight improvement" over the standard DOT-111.

Diluted bitumen spilled into lakes and rivers, contaminating water, soil and sediment and killing wildlife. The derailments, one of which occurred on a bridge over the Makami River, spilling 2.6 million litres, had still not been fully cleaned up three years later, prompting a lawsuit from the Mattagami First Nation with respect to the damage to the river and surrounding areas

According to a report by the Royal Society of Canada, reliable scientific information about the effect of diluted bitumen spills is lacking, and a fragmented system of response plans impedes efforts to prevent and clean up such spills.[1]

The Gogama trains were travelling at speeds well under the Transport Canada-mandated fifty-miles-per-hour limit. The problem was heavy trains meeting weak tracks. A Reuters investigation revealed that a Transport Canada inspection found serious deterioration of the track. A subsequent inspection in July, well after normal speeds had resumed, found continued problems with the tracks. In December 2015, Transport Canada signalled that these problems had been resolved — even though it had not conducted an inspection since the previous July.[2]

The Transportation Safety Board reports on the two derailments, meanwhile, confirmed that in both cases overstressed rails and track joints had gone undetected by insufficiently trained inspectors. The reports also concluded that Transport Canada's speed limits for unit oil trains needed to be lowered. The report on the latter derailment concluded that it was due to an improper rail repair by an inadequately trained inspector.

SAFETY MANAGEMENT SYSTEMS STRENGTHENED?

On April 1, 2015, Transport Canada introduced its new safety management system regulations. They required companies to conduct risk assessments of significant changes to their operations, and to submit them to Transport Canada; to involve workers in the drafting of safety management system plans; and to draft more effective fatigue management plans. Also included were whistleblower protections to encourage employees to report safety concerns.

And finally, seven years after the government-commissioned *Railway Safety Act* Review Panel had recommended them, inspectors would now be able to issue fines — of up to $50,000 for individuals and $250,000 for corporations for actions that threatened safety. Also subject to appeal and delay, it remains to be seen whether this approach is more effective than simply relying on inspector notices and orders.

As for whether money would be put behind good intentions, there were modest increases in money for auditors and engineering staff at the Rail Safety Directorate, but not in operations. At $32 million, the directorate's 2014–15 budget compared poorly with the $42 million allocated (though not fully spent) in 2009–10.

Meanwhile, the Canadian Transportation Agency's budget remained unchanged from before the great oil-by-rail boom, despite its mandate to administer the government's new liability insurance provisions.

A NEW, IMPROVED TANK CAR

Troubled by the petroleum industry's success in pushing back against the Federal Railroad Administration's 2014 attempt to keep volatile components out of oil trains, Transportation Secretary Anthony Foxx took his concerns to the White House. He was to be disappointed again: The Obama administration bowed to industry and state pressure and withdrew the proposed rule. Instead, Washington offloaded the responsibility to North

Dakota to establish the rules. But North Dakota was highly dependent on the oil industry. Its weak regulations permitted significantly higher levels of volatility even than those found on the Lac-Mégantic train.

Just before new railway regulations were announced in May 2015, it was revealed that the departments of transport and energy were launching a joint study into Bakken oil's volatility. Despite all the evidence to the contrary, including multiple explosive train derailments, the petroleum industry was again able to stonewall proposed regulations to remove Bakken crude's components. Ramanan Krishnamoorti, a professor of petroleum engineering at the University of Houston, told Al Jazeera: "The notion that this requires significant research and development is a bunch of BS . . . The science behind this has been revealed over eighty years ago, and developing a simple spreadsheet to calculate risk based on composition and vapour pressure is trivial. This can be done today."

The clearest explanation for the industry's resistance to oil stabilization came from Tony Lucero of oil producer Enerplus, at a hearing of the North Dakota Industrial Commission: "The flammable characteristics of our product are actually a big piece of why this product is so valuable. That is why we can make these very valuable products like gasoline and jet fuel."[3] Because refineries are nearby, there is a ready market for extracted gases in Texas, but there are no refineries in North Dakota, so these volatile gases are shipped across the country dissolved in the crude oil.

On May 1, 2015, Foxx and his Canadian counterpart, Raitt, announced the new TC/DOT-117 design for transporting crude oil and other hazardous products. Following the recommendations of the bilateral task force discussed in Chapter 10, the new tank cars would become mandatory for all new and retrofitted tank cars carrying crude oil when fully phased in by 2025.

The improvements were many: The cars are constructed with thicker steel. They have a thermal protective layer on their interior and a full bumper-like "head-shield" at both ends of the car, top-fitting protection and an enhanced outlet valve handle at the bottom of the tank car to further protect against leakage in the case of a derailment.

Until 2025, the CPC-1232 model — the slightly improved version of the standard DOT-111 — that had been involved in the Gogama crashes would be allowed to carry crude oil and other hazardous products. Canada had advanced the elimination deadline for conventional DOT-111 tank cars carrying crude oil to a year earlier than in the US. Otherwise, the timetable was the same for both countries.

The original government-proposed timetable had called for the complete elimination of the CPC-1232s by 2020, but the Railway Supply Institute, which represented most tank car manufacturers, said the sector could not meet that date. This view was not unanimous amongst manufacturers. Said Greg Saxton of Greenbrier Companies: "If you set a ten-year deadline, it will take ten years. We think that it can be done faster. We don't want to see more Lac-Mégantics."[4] Justin Mikulka, a journalist with online media outlet DeSmog, reported the industry was not exactly hurrying to retrofit its tank car fleet: By mid-2016, only 225 cars out of a fleet of 110,000 had been upgraded.

Foxx also announced a new rule requiring electronic pneumatic brakes on trains carrying dangerous goods to be in place by 2021. Officials accompanying Foxx stressed pneumatic brakes' importance in preventing the pileup of cars upon derailment and warned against delaying its adoption. Secretary Foxx added that electronic pneumatic brakes would have significantly mitigated the consequences of the Lac-Mégantic crash.

Support for the idea came from John Risch of the transportation division of the SMART union, who told a US House of Representatives committee: "I have operated trains with electronic pneumatic brakes and they are the greatest safety advancement I have seen in my forty years in the railroad industry." He went on to explain how these brakes would have prevented the Lac-Mégantic disaster "because when air pressure on a car equipped with electronic pneumatic brakes drops below 50 pounds per square inch, the car automatically goes into emergency mode. So even an improperly secured train will not roll away."

Yet Foxx's new rule was met with a chorus of opposition from the rail and oil lobbies. Even the Railway Association of Canada saw fit to weigh in.

By the same token, railways in both countries have resisted the installation of another safety innovation, positive train control, a remote-control satellite-based system for monitoring and controlling train movements. The National Transportation Safety Board started identifying positive train control as a priority in 1990. A twenty-five-fatality collision between freight and passenger trains in California in 2008 prompted Congress to set a 2015 deadline for the implementation of positive train control for most railroads. Succumbing to industry threats of a total shutdown, Congress pushed the deadline back to December 31, 2018.

When a reporter asked Raitt why her department had not made a similar proposal, Raitt stated she had instructed her officials to find a Canadian solution. Long opposed by Canadian industry, Transport Canada, unlike its US counterpart, had not taken any action to require the implementation of electronic pneumatic brakes or positive train control.

LESSONS STILL IGNORED

In February 2015, CP managers ordered the crew of a train carrying dangerous goods to leave it on the main track atop a steep hill near Revelstoke, B.C., without applying handbrakes. As CBC's Dave Seglins reported, it was a breach of the emergency directive Transport Canada had issued after Lac-Mégantic. The engineer and conductor wanted to secure the train but were overruled by their managers, who wanted the crew's work to be wrapped up before midnight. It was a troubling reminder that the lessons were still being ignored.

In the wake of Lac-Mégantic, Transport Canada committed to strengthening Rule 112 of Canadian Rail Operating Rules, concerning train securement. The Transportation Safety Board had for years recommended that the rule be made more explicit. But in March 2016, the Transportation Safety Board downgraded Transport Canada's progress on improving train securement provisions, noting an increase in runaways since Lac-Mégantic.

The industry had objected strenuously to Transport Canada's emergency directive immediately after the crash, and managed to reverse it, allowing trains to be left unattended for several hours with only the air brakes applied. Prolonged negotiations between Transport Canada and the railways resulted in the final revised Rule 112 coming into force in October 2015, in the twilight of the Harper era. It is still considered problematic by independent experts.

The standard process for changing the Canadian Rail Operating Rules begins with the Railway Association — by itself or in concert with a major railway — drafting the proposed change. Discussion with Transport Canada officials follows. At the end of the day, the transport minister in almost all cases will only accept or reject the railway proposals; there is no middle way. The process occurs behind closed doors, and union input, though required by law, is largely ignored. A letter from Transport Canada to Railway Association CEO Michael Bourque, obtained by *Globe and Mail* reporter Grant Robertson, thanked the lobbyist, notifying him that his proposed revision to the rule was approved.

The new Rule 112, though much more detailed than its predecessor, contains a major flaw, according to Steve Callaghan. It permits a system that layers air brakes and backup devices but does not mandate that handbrakes be applied.

As the Crown's expert witness in the Lac-Mégantic criminal trial, Callaghan concluded that reset safety control systems and air brake systems are not 100 per cent reliable. Callaghan notes: No air brake system in existence retains its brake cylinder air pressure beyond a certain time following an emergency or penalty brake application, and the brake cylinders will eventually leak off. With handbrakes no longer mandatory on non-main tracks, in yards and, under certain conditions, on main tracks either, the revised Rule 112 "leaves the window for another Lac-Mégantic still wide open."

CHAPTER 12
The Civil Lawsuits

In the wake of emergency workers, investigators and politicians, others came to stricken Lac-Mégantic notably, wrongful-death lawyers from south of the border.

Willie Garcia, owner of Texas-based Garcia Law Group PLLC, was on the disaster scene days, if not hours, after the tragedy, as were representatives of two other American wrongful death firms: Meyers & Flowers LLC of Chicago and Webster Law Firm of Houston.

Journalist Sylvie Fournier of *Enquête* chronicled Garcia's story.[1] His firm may represent victims of catastrophic injury, but Garcia himself is not a lawyer but a classic ambulance chaser (or "case runner") who has shown up at major disasters around the world for many years. Enigmatic and discreet, Garcia stays out of the glare of television cameras. Indeed, he was just out of camera during a widely broadcast television interview in Lac-Mégantic with representatives of the two other firms.

Considered one of the best in the business, Garcia presents himself to potential clients with the authority of a lawyer. Pressuring victims' families at their time of greatest vulnerability, he convinces them that he is best suited to get just compensation in US courts. He persuades them to sign an engagement letter — immediately — confirming him as their legal representative.

As of July 24, less than three weeks after the disaster, some victims remained to be identified. But on this date, Garcia reserved a hotel room for a meeting with victims' families.

The Quebec Bar Association, which oversees the province's legal profession, was nowhere in sight to give families advice on their rights and to advise them not to act in haste in the face of these intruders.

Disoriented, in a state of shock, they believed they had no choice but to sign up with Garcia, to whom victims were like meat in a butcher shop, in the words of Texas lawyer Bill Edwards. Pascal Lafontaine, who lost his wife, his brother and sister-in-law in the tragedy, acknowledged that survivors like him were manipulated. He felt betrayed by authorities that there was no one to help them in their time of need. So too did Ginette Cameron, who lost her daughter Geneviève Breton.

There is no evidence Garcia did any work on the case himself other than sign up the "meat" and hand it over to the trial firms — Meyers and Flowers and others — for a fee. The legal agreement, which he cajoled forty families into signing, specified that 40 per cent of the settlement would go to the lawyers. Garcia's finder's fee was estimated to be between $10 million and $15 million.

Two people who committed suicide as a direct result of the disaster were added to the list of wrongful-death claimants: a young firefighter, Kevin Morin, who succumbed to the horror of pulling the remains of his ex-girlfriend out of the rubble; and musician Yvon Ricard, who could not overcome the loss of his close friend and musical partner, Guy Bolduc. The families of these forty-eighth and forty-ninth victims were represented by Mitchell Toups, a Texas attorney.

Meyers and Flowers and Websters handled forty-one of the forty-seven wrongful-death suits filed by the victims' families. The US lawyers engaged a local lawyer, Hans Mercier, to act as an intermediary to navigate the language barrier and the intricacies of Quebec law.

The list of defendants went from one end of the fatal process to the other. They included oil companies: notably World Fuels Services

Inc. and its subsidiary Western Petroleum, Irving Oil, ConocoPhillips, Dakota Plains Holding and its affiliates, and local oil producers. Defendants also included tank car owners and railways, including Montreal, Maine and Atlantic Railway, its owner Rail World, and CP. Given the likelihood of much greater compensation from US courts, the wrongful-death suits were filed in Cook County, Illinois, home of Rail World.

The second civil case, the class-action lawsuit, was filed by Canadian lawyers in the Quebec Superior Court on behalf of Lac-Mégantic individuals and business owners as well as the municipality of Lac-Mégantic, all of which suffered losses relating to the disaster. The attorneys leading the class action were Jeff Orenstein of the Consumer Law Group, Joel Rochon of Rochon Genova LLP and Daniel Larochelle, a Lac-Mégantic lawyer.

Among the defendants there was considerable overlap with the wrongful-death suit. The federal government was added to the list of class-action defendants in February 2014. The lawsuit claimed "Transport Canada was clearly deficient and grossly negligent in its oversight role as it has failed to establish any effective or sustainable oversight approach in the face of Montreal, Maine and Atlantic Railway Canada's open non-compliance with its regulations."[2]

A third legal action arose from Montreal, Maine and Atlantic Railway's August 2013 filing in both Maine and Quebec for bankruptcy protection. Its creditors included the Federal Railroad Administration, the Quebec environment ministry, Rail World, Irving's New Brunswick Southern Railway and CP. Montreal, Maine and Atlantic Railway, which had just $25 million in insurance coverage, sold its assets at auction to New York–based hedge fund Fortress Investment Group in January 2014.

The process to resolve these three legal actions was uniquely complex, requiring collaboration between Canadian and US courts; estates of victims; residents who suffered property damage, employment and business loss, trauma and other health effects; and creditors of the bankrupt company. They involved federal, provincial, state and municipal governments, and Canadian and US-owned companies.

Negotiations to combine the three sets of actions and reach a settlement began in late 2014, co-ordinated by Robert Keach, a Maine attorney appointed Montreal, Maine and Atlantic Railway's trustee by the court. The goal was to reach an arrangement that was satisfactory to the complainants; that would see defendants contributing to a settlement fund and thus be released from further legal liability; and that would permit legal action to continue against defendants who chose not to settle.

In the end, the wrongful-death claimants received $114 million. The individual amounts varied between $400,000 and $5 million, depending on the family situation, with the largest amounts going to children orphaned by the tragedy. The US lawyers received roughly $45 million, 40 per cent of the wrongful-death settlement.

On December 15, 2015, Superior Court Justice Gaétan Dumas approved the settlement covering all three actions and the amounts contributed by the defendants, including the federal government, paving the way for the distribution of the $460-million fund for complainants and creditors.

It was the first in a series of imprints Dumas would leave in sorting out the tragedy of Lac-Mégantic. Dumas also would preside in the 2017 criminal trial against Tom Harding and two other Montreal, Maine and Atlantic Railway employees, Jean Demaître and Richard Labrie, as well as ongoing legal actions against CP.

In addition to the $114 million for victims' families, $317 million was distributed for personal injury, moral damage and economic and property claims from people who lost businesses and jobs, as well as the federal, provincial and local government claims. Roughly $50 million of this was allocated for moral damages, which included claims for post-traumatic stress disorder, bodily injury and inconveniences such as having to be evacuated from the explosion site. About $21 million, 25 per cent of the class-action settlement, was set aside by the judge for lawyers' fees. Roughly four thousand people received cheques from the class-action portion of the settlement fund. As the accounting firm monitoring the Canadian side of the legal proceedings, the Richter Advisory Group distributed settlement money.

While most defendants did not make public the amount they contributed, Irving Oil disclosed its contribution of $75 million, and World Fuels its $135 million. Transport Minister Marc Garneau was unwilling to reveal Ottawa's contribution. But investigative work by law student Valerie Akujobi and Canadian Press reporter Andy Blatchford revealed the number: $75 million. Garneau responded: "We don't acknowledge that we had any responsibility; however, we did want to make a contribution because of the impact of this terrible tragedy in Lac-Mégantic." Bankruptcy trustee Keach contradicted the minister, telling the Canadian Press the contribution was not in fact an altruistic gesture, but rather a move by Ottawa to protect itself against further court action.[3]

Although the payouts made public sound large, they seem less so in light of the bottom lines of the major players involved. World Fuels is a Fortune 500 company with revenues of $30.4 billion US and profits of $861 million US in 2015. Irving Oil is a private, family-owned company with annual revenues estimated at $3 billion to $5 billion. The amounts resemble a cost of doing business more than a deterrent. And in any case, such compensation is often paid out by the companies' insurance. By settling, the companies were protected from further criminal liability and from any further obligation to defend their actions.

THE OCEAN RANGER DIFFERENCE

Why was the Quebec Bar absent as the Texas cowboys took over? The bar claimed that it would have responded had any complaints come forward, but none did. However, *Enquête* discovered that there was in fact an anonymous complaint lodged with the Bar, alleging harassment by the US lawyers and their Quebec co-counsel in the immediate aftermath of the disaster.

The Bar did not launch an investigation into this complaint, which violated its code of conduct. Once *Enquête* brought it to light, the Bar urged victims to file formal complaints so it could launch an investigation. None did, and the Bar left it at that.

This was markedly different from how the lawsuit was conducted for the victims of the Ocean Ranger oil rig sinking off the coast of Newfoundland in 1982. Susan Dodd, who lost her brother in that tragedy, recounts the story in her book, *The Ocean Ranger*. To start, the Ocean Ranger lawsuits were handled in Canada. The defendant company, ODECO, was headquartered in Louisiana, but at the time, the state would not hear cases from non-citizens.

As with Lac-Mégantic, American wrongful death, or tort, lawyers descended on Newfoundland while the search for bodies was still under way, looking to reap 40 per cent of settlements. But in Newfoundland, both politicians and clergy warned the bereaved against entering into any agreements with these US lawyers.

Shortly after the disaster, the Ocean Ranger Families Foundation was formed. Composed of family members, churches and labour representatives, it was a support group, a lobby for safety and a forum for advising and representing the families. Leo Barry, a member of the Newfoundland legislature and himself a personal injuries lawyer, co-ordinated the wrongful-death claims through the foundation's Lawyers Complaints Committee. The committee interviewed eight American tort law firms, from which they selected two. It negotiated the American lawyers down to a portion of an overall fee of 30 per cent of the settlement. In the end, the American lawyers received 16 per cent of the final settlement while the Newfoundland lawyers received 14 per cent.

CANADIAN PACIFIC THE LONE HOLDOUT

Under Hunter Harrison's direction, and presumably with the concurrence of his board — which included former Conservative Transport Minister John Baird — CP, the only defendant named in all three legal actions, refused to settle, insisting it bore no responsibility since its tracks, locomotives and employees were not involved.

As of mid-2018, the class-action lawsuit against CP continues. It alleges CP's liability stems from its partnership with World Fuels and others. It claims that the oil shipment was deliberately misclassified to conceal its volatility. This misclassification allowed the railway company to use older, cheaper tank cars on the "poorly maintained and low-cost" Montreal, Maine and Atlantic Railway route through Maine instead of the much safer CN-owned line along the St. Lawrence's south shore.

Myers and Flowers partner Peter Flowers, acting for most of the wrongful-death complainants, said CP knew the crude oil was unstable before handing it off to an "incompetent" railroad. Calling its refusal to contribute to the settlement fund "reprehensible," Flowers said: "We're going to hold them responsible for what they did in front of the jury of twelve people in the state of Illinois."[4]

Also ongoing is the $409-million Quebec environment ministry creditor lawsuit against CP for cleanup costs, as well as the suit filed by eight insurance companies to reclaim $16.4 million of the funds paid out to their clients after Lac-Mégantic.

Not only did CP not join the settlement arrangement, it tried to torpedo it. After not objecting during almost two years of bankruptcy negotiations, CP filed a motion with the court in June 2015 that the *Companies' Creditors Arrangements Act* did not apply to the case.[5] A month later the Quebec judge Gaétan Dumas rejected CP's motion and ordered the creditor portion of the settlement process to go ahead. CP promptly filed an appeal to the ruling.

According to one of the class-action lawyers, Joel Rochon, CP is determined to drag out the proceedings indefinitely to avoid paying any compensation. A spokesperson put CP's position this way: "We will not contribute to this fund because it frees those parties responsible for the derailment from future liability and legal action, and we continue to contend that we were not among the parties responsible." The trustee Robert Keach responded: "If they really thought that they were completely innocent and that they had no liability, then they would let the distribution proceed and they would defend themselves in court."

In June 2016, the municipality of Lac-Mégantic withdrew its lawsuit against CP on the grounds it would be too costly for the taxpayers of the town because CP would delay indefinitely. The class-action lawyers were dismayed at the optics of the town's withdrawal, which suggested CP is immune from prosecution.

CP filed its defence against the class action in June 2017, claiming that liability was transferred to Montreal, Maine and Atlantic Railway along with the cargo.[6]

The class action against Canadian Pacific, like the wrongful death, insurance company and Quebec environment ministry lawsuits against the company, is due in court in 2019.

CHAPTER 13

The Trial of Tom Harding

On the clear, crisp morning of May 12, 2014, Tom Harding was outside his home in Farnham, working on his boat with his teenage son and a friend.

Suddenly, sirens were screaming, and a Sûreté du Québec SWAT team appeared, dressed in black, with automatic weapons drawn.

Announcing that Harding was charged with criminal negligence causing death, the SWAT team forced all three men to the ground and handcuffed them. Harding was hustled into a black van and driven off.

Why was such extreme action necessary? The reason later given by Sûreté du Québec was that there were allegedly guns in the house, which posed a suicide risk. But Harding's lawyer, Tom Walsh, had, days before, informed the authorities that Harding's only gun had been removed. Walsh also gave the court assurance that, should charges be laid, Harding would surrender himself voluntarily.

Two other men were arrested in similar fashion, and on the same charge: rail traffic controller Richard Labrie and operations director Jean Demaître.

The three men were driven to Lac-Mégantic and marched into the makeshift courtroom, still in handcuffs, in a classic American-style "perp walk" before the duly-informed media and a crowd of onlookers.

The Quebec justice minister said security reasons accounted for this procedure. If, on the other hand, it was a display meant to convince the townspeople that the guilty parties were being brought to justice, it failed. The crowd outside the courtroom was largely quiet. One person cried out, "It's not them that we want." Another remarked to journalists: "I would have expected the minister of transport, who allowed the train to operate with one operator, and the owner of the company to be there in handcuffs." Amir Khadir, member of the Quebec opposition party Québec Solidaire, reflected a widely held view: "[I]t reinforces the perception that justice attacks the weakest, who were responding to orders, and leaves senior officials and executives immune from prosecution."[1] The three men were released on $15,000 bail each.

The crime of criminal negligence causing death carries a maximum penalty of life imprisonment. Harding, the person closest to the event, was widely seen as the most vulnerable.

Curiously, the defunct company Montreal, Maine and Atlantic Railway was also charged with criminal negligence, but not its executives, directors or owner.

EXECUTIVES NOT CHARGED

Why were no criminal negligence charges laid beyond three front-line workers? Amendments to the *Criminal Code*, implemented in 2003 in response to the Westray Mine disaster, state that corporate officers should be held criminally responsible if they know about risks but fail to take appropriate care to eliminate them. In other words, according to law professor Harry Glasbeek, those who create risks to workers and communities have a duty to avert them. According to Glasbeek, the law acknowledges that "the corporation as a legal person, and its directors, executives, managers and employees, as natural persons, could be held accountable for the materialization of risks that they had built into [a] project, and had personally controlled and operationalized."[2]

But Westray lets owners off the hook. Burkhardt, like his Westray counterpart, escaped charges, even though he made all the significant

THE TRIAL OF TOM HARDING   147

operational, policy and investment decisions at Montreal, Maine and

operational, policy and investment decisions at Montreal, Maine and Atlantic Railway, deciding the level of risks to which workers and communities would be exposed. Nothing happened without his permission.

While the prosecutors did not charge Burkhardt nor any Montreal, Maine and Atlantic Railway executive, they did, bizarrely, charge the defunct corporate shell of the railway. The judge at the pre-trial hearing asked the prosecution why the company was being charged, since it could not be jailed.

According to University of Ottawa law professor Jennifer Quaid, it turns out there are two laws: one for employees and one for executives. "Criminal law has a very individualistic sense of causation: that every person makes their own choices — free and rational — and therefore they ought to answer for these choices when they lead to bad things. The law ignores a lot of things that make choices less free — in particular, those things that constrain individual choices [in this case those of the three front-line workers] in ways that suit the prevailing power structures in a neoliberal economy."[3]

In the neoliberal era, the corporation has been vested with the rights of citizenship, gaining, for example, the right of free speech. But somehow these new citizens did not have responsibilities, other than to their shareholders. While company executives could theoretically be charged under the personal responsibility provisions of Westray, the mythical person, the corporation, is a legal entity whose owners could not be put in the dock.

In Glasbeek's words: "Turning the firm into a legal corporation, into an 'ectoplasmic blob,' gets flesh-and-blood capitalists off the market's personal responsibility hook."[4] Corporate law creates a safe haven for owners of capital, who are not subject to the ordinary laws of the market, i.e., personal responsibility.

Both the political and legal actions in the aftermath of Lac-Mégantic have followed a pattern described by legal scholars as pulverization: a process that fragments and decontextualizes events. Glasbeek writes: "The tendency to the pulverization of complex events helps us to understand why regulators and prosecutors are able to concentrate on workers as major culprits rather than on investors who influence managers to force workers to implement profit-seeking activities in circumstances in which obvious risks have not been eliminated."[5]

THE SWISS-CHEESE MODEL

The criminal trial began in a Sherbrooke courtroom on September 11, 2017, more than three years after charges were laid.

The jury ultimately consisted of twelve bilingual jurors — eight men and four women.

The Crown signalled it would call twenty-four civilian witnesses, eleven police witnesses and one expert witness. There were thirty-one days of proceedings over a ten-week period. During this time, the jury listened to detailed testimony, much of it highly technical, at times vague and contradictory. It listened to audio recordings among Montreal, Maine and Atlantic Railway employees, 911 operators, firefighters and Sûreté du Québec.

The witnesses consisted of low-level company or government employees. They included a former Transport Canada inspector, Alain Richer, and former Montreal, Maine and Atlantic Railway employees, including engineer Kevin Mosher — who, as related in Chapter 5, left the company rather than continuing to countenance its slipshod attitude to safety. The most senior company witness to take the stand was Michael Horan, Quebec assistant director of operations. Several firefighters, a taxi driver and police witnesses, including Sûreté du Québec investigators, also appeared.

The expert witness was Steve Callaghan. A native of Sept-Îles, Callaghan had worked on the railway for Quebec North Shore and Labrador Railway. Callaghan later spent ten years as an investigator at the Transportation Safety Board. A respected rail safety authority with a reputation as a straight shooter, Callaghan had been hired by Sûreté du Québec for its investigation.

Lead investigator Mathieu Bouchard was on the case from the outset. While searching the Farnham offices of the Montreal, Maine and Atlantic Railway, Bouchard was working on a computer, copying data.

Suddenly, he noticed the mouse was operating by itself. Or rather, it was being remotely controlled by head office in Maine — an indication, as trial testimony would make clear, of the absolute control it exercised over the Quebec operations.

Sûreté du Québec investigators went to the US five times and met thirty-one US employees and executives of Montreal, Maine and Atlantic Railway, almost all of whom refused to be interviewed and would only communicate through their lawyers. None of the railway executives who were subpoenaed showed up in court. Only one US employee crossed the border to testify: Randy Stahl, supervisor at the Derby, Maine, engine repair shop, where the faulty repair for locomotive 5017 that tipped the dominoes of dysfunction was carried out.

Judge Gaétan Dumas had a reputation for running a tight ship. He regularly ushered the jury out of the courtroom while lawyers challenged evidence, ruling on their challenges and admonishing them when they crossed the line in their interventions.

"It's a trial that should not have happened," Harding's lawyer, Walsh, told reporters at the outset of the trial. The facts of this case did not justify charges of criminal negligence. According to Walsh, the motive was political: to find someone to blame. "Mr. Harding realizes he's partly responsible for a very serious tragedy and that weighs on him a lot more heavily than the trial . . . Is it human error or criminal negligence? That's what this case is about."

The defence requested that the Transportation Safety Board report be admitted in evidence. Transportation Safety Board chair Wendy Tadros had condemned Transport Canada for failing its duty as the guardian of public safety. Employee responsibility, she said, was the last line of defence in railway safety, not a substitute for policy direction, management supervision and government oversight. The judge (and the prosecution), not surprisingly in a criminal law proceeding, sought to narrow the scope of the evidence to the three accused (the pulverization pattern described earlier), ruling that the report was not admissible since it was not deemed to meet the standards required for criminal evidence.

The defendants — on the advice of their lawyers, who determined the Crown had not made a strong enough case — waived their right to mount a formal defence and take the witness stand. In the end, thirty-one of the thirty-six witnesses originally listed by the Crown actually testified.

Lawyers for the Crown made their final arguments, followed by the defence lawyers: Gaétan Bourassa for Demaître, Guy Poupart for Labrie, and Walsh and Charles Shearson for Harding. Their final arguments took eight days, after which the judge gave his instructions to the sequestered jury. Deliberations began January 10. The jury rendered a verdict on January 19.

A few reporters stayed with the case from beginning to end. Others came at key moments: during final arguments and jury deliberations, as tension mounted and the expectation of a verdict — guilty, innocent or a hung jury — drew near.

Shearson delivered the final argument in defence of Harding. In a marathon performance lasting two days, Shearson argued Harding's actions were a departure from the strict provisions of the securement Rule 112, but not one that would constitute criminality. Harding's application of the locomotive air brake and seven handbrakes was more than enough to hold the train, but it wasn't consistent with the handbrake application and efficiency test requirement. "It was not in perfect compliance but it was reasonable," Shearson argued. He noted Callaghan's conclusion was not that Harding caused the accident, but that he did not prevent it.

Shearson used the so-called Swiss cheese model of accident causation to show that a whole series of factors had broken down.[6] If any one of them had not occurred, it would have prevented the runaway. "If" was the key word. If only the engineer could have parked the train on the siding; if only the locomotive engine were not defective or had been removed from its lead position in the convoy; if only the engine did not catch fire, causing the firefighters to turn it off and disable its air brake; if only the engine had been properly wired so as to set off an automatic restart of the automatic air brake system; if only Harding had been allowed by the company to apply the automatic brakes on the tank cars;

if only the rail traffic controller had acquiesced to Harding's wish to go back to the train once the fire was out to make sure it was secured; if only there were another crew member to help diagnose the situation; if only the company had provided proper training to its engineers when embarking on this risky single-person operation; if only a proper risk assessment of this dangerous location had been undertaken; if only the dangerous Montreal, Maine and Atlantic Railway route had not been chosen. If only! Shearson could have extended the Swiss cheese metaphor to policy makers and corporate decision makers going back decades.

At the beginning of his instructions Judge Dumas instructed the jury, laying out a variety of possible verdicts and reminding them that it was in effect three separate trials. With respect to Harding, he told the jury that there were three possible verdicts: guilty of criminal negligence causing death; guilty of a slightly lesser charge of dangerous driving of railway equipment; or not guilty.

During their deliberations, the jury asked for the judge's advice on three occasions. The first time, it asked for clarification on the concept of reasonable doubt. On day six of deliberations, the jury informed the judge that they were at an impasse and asked for his guidance in the event that they could not agree. Dumas instructed them to go back and try again to reach a consensus.

On the final morning, they asked the judge for clarification on how to determine if the actions and decisions of the accused differed from what another employee would have done in the circumstances. The judge reminded the jurors that the prosecution's evidence must show "a marked and substantial departure of what a reasonable person would do." He added: "The fact that someone has failed to comply with a law or regulation cannot invariably lead to the conclusion that he or she has been negligent, or even more, criminally negligent. There must be an appreciation of the entire conduct of the individual placed in context."

Several hours later, the twelve-member jury re-entered the courtroom. After nine days of deliberation, the jury acquitted all three men of criminal negligence.

THE ACCUSED APOLOGIZE

Outside the courtroom, Harding dodged the crush of reporters, too overwhelmed to express his feelings. Walsh said his client was relieved, and his faith in the jury system was affirmed.

Labrie implored reporters: "Could you back up a little bit so I can look at my paper, because my eyes are full of tears." He read a short apology to the people of Lac-Mégantic.

Later that day, a distraught Harding read from a prepared statement: "I cannot find the words sufficiently to express my sympathies. I am deeply sorry for my part of responsibility in this tragedy. I assume this responsibility now, and I will always assume it." It was his first public statement, and his last.

The citizens of Lac-Mégantic were, for the most part, supportive of the verdict.

Jean Clusiault, whose daughter Kathy died in the fire, attended almost every day of the trial. Speaking to reporters outside the courtroom, he praised the decision: "I felt relieved because these are not the right people who should be there."

Julie Morin, the newly elected mayor of Lac-Mégantic, told reporters no one in the community believed the three accused were wholly responsible for the tragedy. She continued: "The Montreal, Maine and Atlantic Railway company had a big role to play in that. It's not just the men who had misjudged; it's the system that's sick." Robert Belle-fleur, spokesperson for the Coalition des Citoyens, elaborated: "The root cause of this deadly tragedy is rather a flagrant lack of systemic vigilance on the part of major players in the oil, rail and government sectors."

In a commentary in *L'Écho de Frontenac*, Gilles Fluet, who was one of the few people who had been close enough to see the train barrelling into town but far enough away to not be killed by it, praised the "professionalism" of the entire trial. His conclusion: "I believe that the three accused, who have endured this ordeal for four and a half years, and who have paid a heavy price, can be considered on the list of victims of this tragedy."

Meanwhile, at the other end of the power spectrum, a statement on the verdict from Transport Minister Garneau was so cautious it did not actually comment on the verdict. "Today we take note of the jury's verdicts in the Lac-Mégantic trial." Garneau said Lac-Mégantic was a reminder of "the importance of having effective legislation and a rigorous enforcement regime."

Quebec's director of criminal and penal prosecutions announced in mid-February that the Crown would not appeal the not-guilty verdict against the three men.

Then, on April 1, two and a half months after the three Montreal, Maine and Atlantic Railway workers were acquitted, the Quebec prosecutor's office announced it was withdrawing its charge of criminal negligence against the railway, ending the charade of charging a defunct corporate entity, without assets, without a lawyer to defend it, with none of its executives or owner charged. None had obeyed the subpoena to come across the border to testify at the trial of the railway workers, nor could they be extradited.

According to the prosecutor's statement, finding the corporation Montreal, Maine and Atlantic Railway criminally liable was absolutely dependent on proving the guilt of individuals associated with the company. The prosecution had chosen to prosecute three low-level employees instead of company decision-makers. Since the minnows were not found guilty, the prosecution argued that it was not worth pursuing the case against the whale.

The question remains: why did they not go after the decision-makers in the first place? Lac-Mégantic was clearly a test case of whether the *Criminal Code* changes made in the wake of the Westray mine disaster would result in charging the company and its executives for the death of forty-seven persons. It clearly failed that test. The prosecution fell back on the usual practice of charging those on the bottom rungs closest to the events.

In response to this decision, Transport Minister Garneau released a statement: "It is the end of a very sad chapter in Canadian history. I think now the Méganticois are looking to the future." Tepid as this language may be, it was saying that this ruling was the end of the line for further proceedings such as a judicial inquiry: time to move on.

OTHER CHARGES AND OUTCOMES

A year after the criminal negligence charges were laid, on June 22, 2015, federal prosecutors laid far less serious penal charges against six Montreal, Maine and Atlantic Railway executives and employees under the *Railway Safety Act* and the *Fisheries Act*. Penalties are minor in comparison to negligence under the *Criminal Code* — a maximum individual penalty of $50,000 and six months in jail.

The charges under the *Railway Safety Act were* for not ensuring the train was properly secured. Three of the six charged were more senior and on the US side of the border (CEO Robert Grindrod, general manager of transportation Lynne Labonté and director of operating practices Kenneth Strout). And three were more junior and on the Quebec side (assistant operations director Mike Horan and two of the men who had faced criminal charges, Harding and Demaître).

The same six persons, plus Labrie, Montreal, Maine and Atlantic Railway's rail traffic controller, were charged under the *Fisheries Act* for polluting Lac-Mégantic and the Chaudière River with a toxic substance.

Montreal, Maine and Atlantic Canada Co. and Montreal, Maine and Atlantic Canada Railway Ltd. were also charged under both acts. The maximum penalty for a company under this act is a $1-million fine. Both charges were redundant for the men facing the possibility of life imprisonment. Here too controlling shareholder Ed Burkhardt escaped prosecution on all penal charges.

In February 2018, the court announced a guilty plea agreement on the penal charges. Five of the individual defendants were fined $50,000 each, and the company $1 million. Labrie was acquitted. Harding was given a six-month conditional prison sentence, to be served in the form of community service.

The company fine was to be taken from undistributed assets from the bankruptcy arrangement. However, at the time of the plea there was only $400,000 in assets set aside in the Montreal, Maine and Atlantic

Railway creditor fund, and the chances of recovering the remaining $600,000 were nil. Moreover, the American executives who pled guilty to these charges cannot be compelled to pay their fines unless they cross the border.

Four years earlier, Transport Canada and the RCMP initiated a joint criminal investigation under the Transportation of Dangerous Goods Directorate, following the Transportation Safety Board revelation that the oil on the train had been misclassified as far less volatile than it actually was. Irving Oil was considered the shipper and therefore liable under the *Act*.

In October 2017, Crown prosecutors announced they had reached a settlement with Irving Oil, which pleaded guilty to thirty-four counts under the *Transport of Dangerous Goods Act* for failing to properly classify the oil and for not properly training its employees in the handling of dangerous goods. The company agreed to pay the government $4 million: $500,000 in fines and a $3.5-million research contribution to Transport Canada to improve the safety of dangerous goods transportation.

The Irving-owned railway, New Brunswick Southern, was charged separately with twenty-four similar counts, including twelve counts of violating the *Transportation of Dangerous Goods Act*, notably its failure to create the proper shipping documents. The other twelve counts relate to unqualified personnel handling dangerous goods. The company has entered a not-guilty plea. A trial date was set for March 25, 2019.

JUSTICE DENIED

All criminal and civil actions have been settled behind closed doors without going to trial except the criminal charges against Harding and his fellow workers. The only people who testified were low-level company and government employees, and police investigators. No company executives; no senior government officials, especially those who made and approved the decision to allow Montreal, Maine and Atlantic Railway to operate its trains with single-person crews; no politicians responsible for transportation policy and overall regulatory and budgetary policy; no industry leaders — none of them were compelled to testify. As a vehicle to uncover the truth, the legal system failed miserably.

In April 2018, following the failure of all criminal negligence proceedings to reach a guilty verdict, the National Assembly of Quebec passed a unanimous resolution calling on the federal government to hold a commission of inquiry. Both Prime Minister Trudeau and Transport Minister Garneau rejected the demand.

CHAPTER 14

The Four Tragedies of Lac-Mégantic

The death of forty-seven people and the destruction of the town's heart did not end the anguish of Lac-Mégantic. That was, in fact, only the beginning. As local activists put it, what unfolded in Lac-Mégantic was a series of cascading tragedies.

That victims' families should become prey for legal predators, as related in Chapter 12, was the second tragedy after the initial disaster.

Next came the third and fourth tragedies — both of them ways, one unexpected, that the community was still suffering five years after the inferno.

The expected tragedy was the effect on citizens' health.

The first annual survey by the Eastern Townships regional public health authority, at the University of Sherbrooke, conducted in 2014, found that two-thirds of the Lac-Mégantic population were experiencing symptoms of post-traumatic stress disorder, high levels of anxiety and depression and excessive medication and drug use.[1] Half continued to experience symptoms of trauma in 2017.

Trauma among those most directly exposed to the disaster — people who lost friends, family, homes and jobs — was especially high: 76 per cent in 2015, and still 58 per cent in 2017. A joint study by the University of Sherbrooke and the University of Quebec at Chicoutimi found that 40 per cent of youth under twenty-five who were highly exposed to the tragedy had contemplated suicide in 2017, and were twice as likely as the average Quebec youth to self-mutilate.

Six million litres of Bakken oil disgorged from the tank cars — the largest land-based oil spill in North American history. Most of the oil burned, but large amounts poured into the local waterways and soil. Highly toxic petroleum hydrocarbon compounds, including benzene, toluene, dioxins and furans, were released into the air, water and soil. These pollutants are all known to affect human, animal and plant life. The firefighters who battled the blaze experienced prolonged exposure to the hydrocarbons during the fire, but they have not been properly monitored to assess the effects on their health over time.

In the weeks and months following the disaster, environmental teams worked to stem the oil flow. Booms were deployed, and pumping operations retrieved about half the estimated hundred thousand litres of oil that spilled into the Chaudière River. Floating oil was detected 185 kilometres away, where the river empties into the St. Lawrence. Several municipalities along the route were forced to find alternative water sources well into the fall of 2013. Cleaning techniques developed from the Exxon Valdez spill were applied to some forty kilometres of shoreline. Oil also penetrated deep into the sediment at the river bottom. Over time, excavation crews removed rubble and soil from the disaster zone. In all, 267,000 tonnes of contaminated soil were removed, and 62 million litres of water were treated.

Rosa Galvez, a Laval University professor and one of Canada's leading experts on pollution control and human health, was vacationing at Lac-Mégantic on July 6 when disaster struck. Galvez independently conducted in-depth studies of the environmental impact of the disaster.[2] Her research suggests the hydrocarbons are interacting with the water, contaminating the food chain. Noting that no study of their cumulative impact or eco-toxicity has yet been done, Galvez has questioned the wisdom of continuing to transport unconventional oil by rail, especially through populated areas. (Galvez was appointed to the Senate in 2016.)

MESMERIZED BY OUTSIDERS

The final tragedy of Lac-Mégantic was that what should have been a balm — the rebuilding of the town's heart — did not heal but added more injury. The process evokes Naomi Klein's book *The Shock Doctrine: The Rise of Disaster Capitalism*, which documents how victims of disasters are victimized a second time by powerful interests using the crisis to advance their own agendas.

Klein studied disasters around the world, from the US invasion of Iraq to the Sri Lankan tsunami to Hurricane Katrina in New Orleans. In each case, those seizing control are able to impose shock-therapy "solutions" upon a community that is in crisis, hence unable to resist policies that in normal times would not pass.

Chapter 12 described the story of "case runner" Willie Garcia, who was on the disaster scene almost immediately, persuading grieving family members to sign up with him for an exorbitant share of the wrongful-death compensation. No one else in a position of power — not government, not the legal profession — stepped in to prevent the exploitation.

But Garcia and the cohort of wrongful-death litigators were not the only ones to benefit from the disaster. Many citizens have felt betrayed by local politicians who were mesmerized by outsiders who came with grandiose plans for reconstruction and visions of a new twenty-first-century community, erasing the town's identity.

While many people have given in to despair and passivity, Lac-Mégantic's is also a hopeful story of many who have resisted the downward spiral. In the months following the tragedy, citizens groups banded together, calling attention to the condition of the tracks that run through town and pushing for a bypass. Others focused on the environmental damage resulting from the disaster, and the town's reconstruction efforts.[3]

The largest citizens group, the *Coalition des citoyens et des organismes engagés pour la securité ferroviare de Lac-Mégantic*, became known as the Coalition des Citoyens.[4] They continue to fight tirelessly on behalf of their community, in the face of enormous odds and with virtually no resources. In addition to Robert Bellefleur, its founder and main spokesperson, the core team consists of André Blais, Gilbert Carette, Gilles Fluet, André Lachapelle, Richard Poirier and Claude Roy, as well as Jacques Gagnon from a sister coalition. It also includes Dr. Richard Lefebvre from nearby St.-Romain, and Nicole Jetté, from St.-Hyacinthe.[5]

Bellefleur would have been at the Musi-Café on the night of July 5, 2013, had not work duties taken him to Sherbrooke. Bellefleur traces the birth of the Coalition to April 2014, when he was informed by a municipal official that the death train could have just as easily derailed not at the curve downtown but at another bend — the one near where Bellefleur lived on the outskirts of town.

Troubled by this information, Bellefleur walked up behind his house. There he observed a track in an advanced stage of decay. Worse, he knew that the company taking over from Montreal, Maine and Atlantic Railway, Central Maine & Quebec Railway would soon resume transporting dangerous goods.

He was shaken. Images of the disaster swelled back into his mind. He had trouble sleeping. He sent photos to his local councillor, who informed him that he, too, was worried, but powerless to do anything. Bellefleur then contacted Transport Canada, which did not return his calls.

Bellefleur began knocking on doors, looking for others who shared his concern. The Coalition was soon formed.

Its members walk the tracks — defying threats of prosecution for trespassing from the Central Maine & Quebec Railway — monitoring track conditions and alerting the public to the ever-present safety risks as dangerous goods continue to pass through the town. They question Central Maine & Quebec's parking, switching and securement practices, as well as its claims that the track has been fully repaired. They engage regularly with Transport Canada officials, questioning its safety oversight and enforcement practices. They challenge the Quebec environment ministry's efforts to downplay the contamination caused by the disaster. They hold press conferences and organize petitions, marches and demonstrations; they challenge local, provincial and federal politicians and participate in town halls, forums and conferences.

They have fought relentlessly for a rail bypass and for rail safety. They continue to press for a judicial inquiry into the disaster, asking why those responsible continue to escape accountability.

A BONANZA OF DESTRUCTION

Liette Gilbert teaches in the Faculty of Environmental Studies at York University in Toronto. She has deep ties to Lac-Mégantic, having grown up in Nantes. Gilbert has written about the "creative destruction that shaped the reconstruction effort in Lac-Mégantic, describing how those in control manipulated the language of urgency, risk and resilience to impose their agenda on a traumatized community."[6]

Federal and provincial governments contributed, I estimate, roughly $600 million to fund the decontamination, cleanup and reconstruction of the town. It was a bonanza for private contractors eager to get a piece of the action. They quickly allied themselves with municipal politicians and those in charge of the project.

In September 2013, the Quebec government passed Bill 57, allowing Lac-Mégantic, in the midst of dealing with the crisis, to postpone municipal elections. It also gave the municipal council carte blanche to expedite planning decisions, demolish buildings and expropriate property as part of the rebuilding and "normalization process." The council was granted the power to demolish any building in the "containment zone" that it deemed unfit for habitation due to contamination.

Golder Associates was initially engaged by Montreal, Maine and Atlantic Railway for the cleanup effort. But after the railway declared bankruptcy, the Quebec government hired Pomerleau Inc. to oversee both the excavation and removal of contaminated soil and debris and the rebuilding of tracks, utilities and sewer lines.

Golder, still on retainer, assessed the extent of contamination of the remaining buildings in the containment zone. Its confidential report submitted in November 2013 — obtained by activist Jonathan Santerre under access to information law — found that of the thirty-nine buildings still standing, only seven were contaminated by the oil spill, five were historically contaminated and twenty-seven had no contamination at all. At the end of December, the newly elected Liberal provincial government hired the Fortune 500 engineering firm AECOM to take over the management of the effort.

The municipal council's first project, Promenade Papineau, relocated destroyed businesses, including Musi-Café, into newly constructed buildings close to the tracks but oddly isolated from the town's original location.

Its second project was to demolish a historic church and expropriate residences and businesses in Fatima parish to make way for new locations of prominent Quebec companies — pharmacy Jean Coutu, grocer Metro and Banque Nationale.

Some fifty residents had their property expropriated in this project. Many got visits from realtors who represented the stores, making offers for their property — and threatening them that if they did not accept the offer, the municipal council would expropriate it for even less.

A sawmill, Billots Select, resisted for several months, but in the end, it too was expropriated. It all happened quickly, leaving residents scant opportunity to question and mobilize against the plan.

The stores were built with the help of tax credits paid for out of the Avenir Lac-Mégantic Fund. It was a questionable use of a fund established with individual donations from across the country in the wake of the tragedy.

Rebuilding the tracks was deemed a matter of urgency by the business community and municipal officials — it was crucial to get the always train-dependent town economy back on its feet. Pomerleau rebuilt the track at its original location, though it was later discovered that the deadly curve where the derailment occurred was reconstructed to make an even sharper turn. By November 2013, the train was up and running again, though not carrying dangerous goods for another year.

Outspoken citizen Paul Dostie testified about the traumatic impact of the trains' reappearance before a Quebec environmental consultation regarding various rail bypass scenarios: "Here the trains no longer whistle: They scream . . . At night, I hear the brakes of the cars squeal . . . above the wheels, there are and will be dozens of tank cars loaded with propane gas, sulfuric acid and other toxic products. I also hear locomotives shouting their priority at level crossings and engines rumble when they pull the heavy convoys. The dishes in the cupboard tremble."

Town officials deployed a narrative of healing as well as of physical rebuilding. It launched a citizen-participation process Réinventer la ville to guide the reconstruction of the town. But in reality the process was conducted within parameters predetermined by the creative destruction proponents.

In the final consultation session, just before the first anniversary of the tragedy, residents stated clearly that they did not want to see any more buildings expropriated. There was a strong consensus to preserve thirty of the thirty-nine buildings in the containment zone. They wanted the town rebuilt in a recognizable image of what they had known.

However, for the group driving the reconstruction effort — municipal, provincial and federal politicians; private contractors; finance and insurance officials and promoters — the citizens' consultation did not accord with their vision of a clean slate, a twenty-first-century version of the historic town. It was a vision that even included far-fetched proposals for a catastrophe-tourism project akin to the one mounted in New York after 9/11.

Town council decided on October 29, 2014, to destroy thirty-six of the thirty-nine containment-zone buildings, citing a lingering risk of contamination — despite the assessment from Golder to the contrary. The three buildings left standing were the City Hall and its adjacent fire hall, the Bell Canada building and the railway station.

More buildings were destroyed in this exercise than in the fire.

Owners of the targeted buildings were given dire accounts of the degree of contamination and told to either accept the town's offer or see their properties expropriated. Even after the demolition and decontamination, the municipality could not guarantee to the buyers of these properties that the land had been completely decontaminated. Any cost of further analysis toward rehabilitation would have to be borne by the buyer itself.

In December 2014, the town awarded two contracts for demolition, excavation, decontamination and environmental rehabilitation of the site to a local contractor, Lafontaine & Fils. The work was to be undertaken during the winter and spring of 2015, so reconstruction could begin as quickly as possible.

If businesses were treated with a sort of rough justice in the rebuilding process, people whose homes were destroyed had it even rougher.

Geneviève Boulanger and her family lost everything on July 6. Yet the subsequent months of uncertainty and their struggle to recover their land were a thousand times worse than all their material losses, Boulanger said.

Their family home by the lake was destroyed by the fire, but the land, though in the containment zone, was not contaminated by the spill, according to the expert assessment. They wanted to rebuild and remain as part of a downtown neighbourhood community, as did many citizens who participated in the consultation process. "Our main intention was to rebuild our home, to continue raising our children there," Boulanger said. "But we continued to face obstacles. We had to work hard, write letters and articles, give interviews, speak at public meetings — even though we were already completely exhausted by this ordeal."

Representatives of the town and Quebec's environment ministry met privately with those whose homes had been destroyed, urging them to sell, according to Boulanger. Many would be intimidated into accepting the offer. Boulanger and her family were the only ones who succeeded in reclaiming their land and rebuilding their home on its original site.

Calling it the oldest trick in the creative destruction playbook, Gilbert wrote:

> The discourse of risk was indeed used to stigmatize,
> devalue and condemn remaining properties and to justify a
> ready-to-build clean slate that would appeal to developers,
> investors, bankers and insurers. In a small town facing
> depopulation, financial deficits and limited growth, the

use value of city structures was literally demolished to make place for exchange value and capital accumulation. Emotional attachment was bulldozed in favour of capital investments. Ultimately, displaced residents and business people absorbed the risks so that investors, developers and insurance companies would not have to.

Jonathan Santerre, creator of Le Carré Bleu Lac-Mégantic Facebook page, was less restrained in his summary of what happened: Use a disaster to steal territory, restrict citizens' rights and freedoms, impose new emergency laws, offer a buffet to the private sector, abuse power and undermine democracy for personal agendas of the elite or politicians.

Needless to say, it didn't look that way to those driving the process. Speaking to Global News in October 2017, the municipal director general of Lac-Mégantic, Marie-Claude Arguin, expressed skepticism regarding the results of studies demonstrating widespread trauma amongst citizens. She said people had been coming to her, saying, "Why don't I have the symptoms? I must not have a heart." She believes that the population is doing a lot better than is indicated by the public health studies. A campaign to encourage positivity and resilience — a buzzword often invoked throughout the reconstruction process — is needed. People are ready to move on.

But if resilience is about resourcefulness and the ability to bounce back, it often omits question: "Bounce back to what?" According to Gilbert, a more critical view sees "resilience" as a feint to appease and silence demands for accountability and rationalize the process of creative destruction.

Fluet, who underwent months of psychological counselling after the disaster, disputes the view that those who support the reconstruction effort are, by definition, the resilient ones. However, he counts himself among those who, with limited means at their disposal, try to see clearly, question authority and remain vigilant. They represent an alternative definition of resilience.

CHAPTER 15
Plus ça Change

The Lac-Mégantic disaster posed a question for Canada. Could the country arrest the withdrawal, orchestrated by alternating Conservative and Liberal governments over thirty-plus years, from protecting the public?

Five years after the disaster, deregulation and deference to industry are still the order of the day. As the following survey shows, reports and recommendations on safety abound, but actual improvements are harder to find.

ONE-FOR-ONE RULE STILL THE CENTREPIECE OF LIBERAL REGULATORY POLICY

The new Liberal regulatory policy, the Cabinet Directive on Regulatory Policy, which comes into effect in the fall of 2018, is not a significant departure from the Harper policy. The one-for-one rule is still in place.

A report from the Finance department's (Business) Advisory Council on Economic Growth identifies priorities for establishing what it calls an agile regulatory system: consistency with competitiveness, innovation and business investment imperatives; and compatibility with other regulatory jurisdictions. Regulations' impact on health, safety and the environment is not mentioned. A regulatory review of key sectors including transportation is planned for the next three years based on the report's priorities.

TRUDEAU GOVERNMENT SEE-SAWS ON SAFETY FUNDING

On the campaign trail in 2015, the Liberal team led by Justin Trudeau promised to provide Transport Canada with enough funding to tighten up rail safety. But since they were elected, the record of Trudeau's Liberals on this file has been indifferent. The government's first two years saw funding go up, then drop in subsequent years, according to the departmental plan. Transport Canada's overall spending on "transportation safety and security" was projected to fall by over 17 per cent between 2018–19 and 2020–21. The department's numbers say the number of inspectors has been hiked. But observers say the additions are mainly desk jobs, not personnel in the field, where transgressions happen.

NEW TANK CARS ARE COMING, SLOWLY

In July 2016, Transport Minister Marc Garneau moved up the cut-off date for transporting crude in standard DOT-111 tank cars to November 1 of that year. While the move was praised by Transportation Safety Board chair Kathy Fox for highlighting "Canadian leadership" on tank-car safety, there was less to the news than met the eye.

Garneau failed to mention that the CPC-1232 model — a "slightly improved" DOT-111 — would still be allowed to carry crude until May 1, 2025. Then they would be fully replaced by the newly designed TC/DOT-117.

Yet according to a US Department of Transport report, in all of North America there were only 360 legacy DOT-111 tank cars still carrying crude oil in 2016. The vast majority of the old DOT-111 fleet was carrying ethanol, and thus was not affected by Garneau's accelerated phase-out.

The Transportation Safety Board had warned that the CPC-1232 phase-out was too long. But an internal Transport Canada memorandum to Garneau cautioned that accelerating the schedule was not feasible, considering economic realities and that any change "would require US regulatory support." The US tank car industry was pushing back strongly, claiming there was insufficient manufacturing capacity to meet a tighter deadline. Such were the limits within which Canadian regulators were permitted to reduce risk to the public.

In any case, the TC-117 is not a cure-all. As we've seen, the vast majority of bitumen transported by rail is in diluted form — dilbit or synbit. Highly volatile components are added to the raw bitumen to make it flow. The TC-117, while safer than existing models, is not designed with bitumen in mind.

It is much safer to transport bitumen in its raw form in tank cars specially outfitted with steam coils to maintain its fluidity. However, relatively few of these specialized cars have been built, and so only a fraction of bitumen is transported in raw form. The TC-117, which is expected to carry the vast majority of bitumen into the future, is not fitted with steam coils.

Eighteen months prior to Garneau's announcement came the two CN diluted-bitumen train derailments near Gogama, Ontario, described in Chapter 11. This should have been a red flag. And if that wasn't sufficient, more troubling was the June 2018 incident in which a Burlington Northern Santa Fe train hauling diluted bitumen from Alberta in retrofitted CPC-1232 tank cars rebuilt to the state-of-the-art TC/DOT-117 standard derailed near the Little Rock River, Iowa. Fourteen cars punctured, spilling over 871,000 litres of bitumen.

SAFETY MANAGEMENT SYSTEMS ARE STILL LAGGING

It fell to the Liberal government to ensure that new safety management system regulations, which came into effect just months before the Harper era ended, were properly implemented. Transportation Safety Board chair Kathy Fox, speaking to a National Railway Day conference in November 2017, complained that companies were still not taking their risk assessment obligations seriously: "There are still railway companies that aren't conducting risk assessments before making operational changes. Moreover, there still seems to be an attitude of trying to justify why a risk assessment is not required by the regulation."

Among the new safety management system regulations are those requiring that work-rest scheduling practices be compatible with the science of fatigue management. But Steve Callaghan, the expert witness at the criminal trial, calls these regulations "a farce." Companies have avoided re-examining their work-rest scheduling practices simply because of the costs involved, and because regulations allow them to do so, says Callaghan. Currently, train crews are exempt from the *Canada Labour Code*'s maximum-hours-of-work provisions.

In 2016, company resistance and Transport Canada inaction prompted the Transportation Safety Board to put fatigue management on its watchlist for the first time, stating that Transport Canada has been aware of the problem for many years but was continuing to drag its feet. It added that sleep-related fatigue has been a cause or risk factor in one-fifth of Transportation Safety Board accident investigations over the last two decades.

Transport Canada and Minister Garneau say they are on the case.

EMERGENCY PREPAREDNESS

One of the lessons of Lac-Mégantic was that firefighters, especially from small communities, lacked the training to handle such large-scale accidents. They lacked experience with specialized equipment and knowledge of available emergency response resources.

The federal government's Emergency Response Task Force, convened in the months following Lac-Mégantic, issued its final report to the Transportation of Dangerous Goods Directorate in July 2016. It contained thirty-three recommendations. They included: The specification of the contents of emergency response assistance plans and company reporting requirements; the specification of inspector reporting procedures; improved outreach and communication activities, and information sharing with other departments and agencies; the additional mapping of routes of flammable liquids transported by rail; and the creation of specialized training programs. Transport Canada has made significant progress implementing the task force's recommendations.

The jury is still out on whether these changes will be effective. In the meantime, municipal first responders and emergency planners are still being denied real-time information about dangerous goods passing through their communities.

RAILWAY SAFETY ACT REVIEW RECYCLED

At the behest of Minister Garneau, an independent commission conducted an accelerated review of the *Railway Safety Act*. It was the first since the Harper government's 2007 *Railway Safety Act* review, on the eve of the oil-by-rail boom.

Its report, issued in May 2018, made sixteen recommendations. Many, such as calls for improved fatigue management, the study of electronic braking systems and that Transport Canada strengthen its capacity in the development and adoption of rail safety technology, were recycled in various forms from the previous review. Overall, the effort opted for a series of marginal recommendations, papering over fundamental flaws in the railway safety regime, above all the power relationship between the industry and Transport Canada.

But if the report was a missed opportunity, it did resurrect, if inadvertently, the problem of rail safety statistics, even if it conveniently overlooked some of the negative trends in rail safety since Lac-Mégantic.

The 2007 review noted a "widely held view that the Transportation Safety Board's published data on railway occurrences did not provide a comprehensive or fully accurate picture of railway safety in Canada." These statistics remain unreliable in large part because of the non-reporting of accidents. In a post-Mégantic audit, the Transportation Safety Board learned of more than 250 accidents that had not been reported between 2007 and 2013.

Moreover, this data was not collected systematically. The Transportation Safety Board looked at seven years of CN data, but only thirteen months of CP records (even that small sample showed one hundred accidents). For Montreal, Maine and Atlantic Railway, the Transportation Safety Board only considered data from 2010 to 2013. It found that for every accident Montreal, Maine and Atlantic Railway reported in the years before Lac-Mégantic, it experienced another two that it did not report. Finally, a CN audit between 2001 and 2007 added between two hundred and four hundred accidents per year to the numbers.

Jennifer Winter, with the School of Policy Studies at the University of Calgary, wrote a sharp critique of rail safety data in 2014: "When Canadians ask, as many have in recent months, whether the rail transport system is 'safe,' they surely want to know whether the accident rate is low — compared to other countries and other forms of transport — and whether it has been improving or getting worse over time. Yet the statistics that might provide the answer are worryingly inaccessible, sometimes conflicting and in certain cases not available at all."[1]

FREEDOM OF INFORMATION NOT IMPROVING
Among the Trudeau government promises of "real change" was a more transparent government. Trudeau's mandate letter to Transport Minister Garneau read: "Government and its information should be open by default."

This was a breath of fresh air for an author frustrated by the Harper government's procrastination and lengthy delays in providing information about Transport Canada's role in the Lac-Mégantic disaster.

Yet things did not change — for this book, or overall. A freedom-of-information audit conducted by the University of King's College concluded that "the Liberal government's performance was even worse than in the latter years of the former Stephen Harper government."[2] This is startling, considering the Harper government was considered the most secretive since the legislation was first introduced more than three decades ago. Or perhaps it was an example of something that has become mundane in the neoliberal era: The way regressive tactics, once discovered, stay in the bloodstream of politics even when governments change stripe.

THE TRUMP EFFECT HAS YET TO HIT

The attack of the Trump administration on regulation could fill a good-sized book, or several of them. The climate was bad for rail safety, and so was the weather. Any forward-looking effort that came up for consideration was batted back.

A case in point is the rule requiring minimum two-member crews for all train operations, proposed by the Federal Railroad Administration in the last months of the Obama administration. The railways immediately demanded that the proposal be withdrawn. Edward Hamberger, CEO of the Association of American Railroads, called it "a textbook example of unnecessary regulation . . . With no data showing that one-person operations compromise safety, there is no basis — other than anecdotal storytelling — for enacting a general prohibition on crew size reductions."[3]

The Federal Railroad Administration delayed issuing the final rule. Once in office, Trump immediately sent the rule back to the administration for internment in regulatory purgatory.

This was cheered by the Canadian railway industry, which has been pushing hard behind the scenes for the elimination of the post Lac-Mégantic operating rule that trains carrying dangerous goods must have at least two employees.

The same inclination affected positive train control, the remote-control satellite-based protection system long advocated by the National Transportation Safety Board. In the wake of a fatal California train crash, Congress in 2008 passed legislation setting a 2015 deadline for the implementation of the technology. It subsequently extended the deadline to the end of 2018.

A passenger train accident near Tacoma, Washington, in November 2017 killed three and injured dozens more. A positive train control system would have prevented the accident (one was installed after the fact). But under the Trump administration, the deadline for across-the-board positive train control implementation has been put off indefinitely.

The Federal Railroad Administration had also imposed a rule that unit trains carrying high-hazard liquids must be operated with an electronically controlled pneumatic braking system by 2021.[4] As I described in Chapter 11, electronically controlled pneumatic brakes are widely seen as a quantum leap in rail safety. Again, the industry lobby, including the Railway Association of Canada, pushed back, arguing that the technology had only marginal safety benefits and would cause operating disruptions. Nevertheless, the Federal Railroad Administration upheld its rule change.

But as the Trump administration's first year drew to a close, the Department of Transportation announced that this timeline too would be erased. Also removed were prospective regulations to address track deterioration and to require engineers to be screened for sleep apnea, which the National Transportation Safety Board had found to be a cause in at least thirteen accidents it investigated.

The Trump deregulation tsunami will put intense pressure on regulators in Canada to follow suit in a downward spiral of "harmonization." The ground has already been softened up. At the top of the Canadian American Business Council's wish list for the NAFTA renegotiation was regulatory harmonization. Exactly the same message was sounded by the Trudeau government's Advisory Council on Economic Growth.

Canadian-based companies will argue that following Trump's lead is necessary to maintain their competitiveness under NAFTA, given that 35 per cent of Canadian railway revenue comes from cross-border trade, and 79 per cent of Canada's crude oil production is exported to the US.

Public input is nominally part of the regulatory harmonization process within the bilateral Regulatory Cooperation Council, but in reality it is a closed-door business-government exercise. The larger partner is in the driver's seat. Canada, with some exceptions, usually adopts US regulatory standards, not the other way around.

MONTREAL, MAINE AND ATLANTIC RAILWAY GETS A SUCCESSOR

Fortress Investment Group, a publicly traded New York–based investment company, won the auction for Montreal, Maine and Atlantic

Railway's assets in January 2014, bidding almost $16 million US. It began operations six months later. A similar operation to Pershing Square Capital Management, which took control of CP in 2012, Fortress was named Hedge Fund Manager of the Year by *Institutional Investor* magazine in 2012.

Fortress renamed the company Central Maine & Quebec Railway, and slotted it into its transportation and infrastructure division, which also managed several US railways. John Giles, a forty-five-year railroad veteran, was lured out of retirement and appointed CEO, again echoing the Pershing Square-CP narrative.

The company committed to investing $23 million US in track and infrastructure improvements, $10 million of it on the Quebec leg. (The work on the American side was subsidized by the Maine and federal governments.) It also replaced all the locomotives that belonged to its previous owner. Having completed renovations by the end of 2014 and obtained the approval of Transport Canada, the Central Maine & Quebec Railway began hauling dangerous goods at the beginning of 2015.

Giles told the *Bangor Daily News*: "We patched up the track, and then we negotiated what we call a social compact with the city of [Lac-] Mégantic, and that was something we thought was necessary because those people had been through so much."[5]

Although it began shipping dangerous goods in 2015, at the town's request Central Maine & Quebec declared a moratorium on transporting crude oil through the town. Relations were good, according to Conrad Lebrun, director of buildings and projects for Lac-Mégantic: "We have access to Central Maine & Quebec representatives. When we need to, we call them and they call us right back and we work issues out well. We expect it to keep going in the future."

However, in the months that followed, Robert Bellefleur and the Coalition des Citoyens were still concerned about the state of the track, which they continued to monitor, discovering signs of disrepair. The daily passage of trains carrying hazardous products — sulphuric acid, propane, sodium chloride and ethanol — through the heart of town was worrisome.

In July 2015, on the second anniversary of the tragedy, the Coalition asked independent railway expert Jacques Vandersleyen to accompany them on an inspection of the tracks. Vandersleyen was shocked by what he saw: The condition of the tracks was, in his view, unsafe for transporting dangerous goods. Transport Canada responded that this portion of the track had been inspected in May and that its experts considered it safe. The next day the mayor requested an independent evaluation of the track.

The Coalition, frustrated at the inaction and non-responses from the company and Transport Canada, sent a letter to CEO Giles in September, copied to Transport Minister Lisa Raitt — with a petition from 2,600 residents asking the town council to seek an injunction to stop the company from carrying dangerous goods until it had fully completed its track repairs. The council did not, however, proceed with the injunction, nor did it undertake its promised independent evaluation of the track, given that it would cost more than $25,000.

Less than two years after it began operations in 2014, Central Maine & Quebec had more than doubled its traffic from three thousand carloads per quarter to almost seven thousand; in 2016 it posted its first profit.[6]

According to an assessment by *Forbes* magazine, Fortress has been a growth dynamo led by its transportation division, tripling revenues between 2014 and 2016. A *Forbes* analyst praised "the explosive growth potential of this extremely niche but lucrative opportunity."[7] US trade publication *Railway Age* awarded Central Maine & Quebec its 2016 Regional Railway of the Year award. It was the same publication that had celebrated Ed Burkhardt, Hunter Harrison and Paul Tellier.

In December 2017, SoftBank Group Corp. acquired Fortress Investments for $3.3 billion US. SoftBank is a Japanese-owned global investment conglomerate that *Forbes* rates as the thirty-eighth-largest public company in the world. Its distant, complex ownership structure would blur even further the accountability lines in the event of another catastrophic event.

A FIX FOR LAC-MÉGANTIC

In April 2016, Transport Minister Garneau visited Lac-Mégantic, accompanied by John Giles, CEO of Central Maine & Quebec, to assure the community that the track through town was safe and that rail safety was his number-one priority. Paul Dostie told Garneau that lost trust is hard to recover: "You talk about safety; it does not assuage me. It is like telling a child who has been disfigured by a dog to go walk the dog."

The Coalition asked Garneau to order Central Maine & Quebec to stop switching and parking railcars at the very location from which the fateful train had run away. (The new operator was doing so because Montreal, Maine and Atlantic Railway's old rail yard, destroyed in the fire, was appropriated by the municipality.) The Coalition repeated its request that Garneau order the company to fix its tracks, especially because the curve where the train had derailed was now even sharper.

Garneau replied that such matters were up to the company. This did not instill confidence in the Coalition, whose members renewed their efforts, with measures such as a press conference on Parliament Hill and Bellefleur confronting Prime Minister Trudeau at a town hall in Sherbrooke. Bellefleur also addressed the commission reviewing the *Railway Safety Act*, concluding with a chilling question: "If we tolerate such risk factors in Lac-Mégantic, the site of the most destructive railway tragedy in Canadian history, what is happening elsewhere in Canada?"

Bellefleur's concern was based on his own continuing observations. He was driving back from the criminal trial of Harding et al. late one night in October 2017 when he noticed a convoy of railcars parked on the main track at Nantes without a locomotive or a derailer. His attempt to raise this with Transport Canada eventually produced the answer that Central Maine & Quebec was not breaking any rule. On February 3, 2018, Bellefleur noticed a fifty-car convoy with twenty-nine tank cars of propane — which is highly explosive — in the same location. It was there for about thirty-five minutes without a locomotive, unattended, without a derail device and without handbrakes.

Government, at least, was working on one solution for Lac-Mégantic.

On the morning of May 11, 2018, Prime Minister Trudeau, Transport Minister Garneau and Quebec Premier Philippe Couillard announced, with the gaping vacant space that had once been Lac-Mégantic's town centre behind them, that they would fund a 12.8-kilometre bypass around the town at an estimated cost of $133 million. Ottawa and Quebec City would share the cost sixty-forty.

The bypass construction will be managed by Central Maine & Quebec, and the track will be owned by the company upon completion. Ownership of the original track property, estimated to be worth less than $1 million, will revert to the government. Construction, it was said, will start in 2019 and be completed in 2022.

The mayors of the neighbouring towns of Frontenac and Nantes were critical of the selected route and proposed a modified version. Mayors of twenty communities in the region sent a letter to the provincial and federal governments requesting that they accommodate this variation. It was rejected. Bellefleur, relieved that after years of advocacy the bypass would finally go forward, was nevertheless troubled by the fact that it would create divisions at a moment that should be a coming together and healing of the communities.

FIFTH ANNIVERSARY BOMBSHELL

Just days before the fifth anniversary of the Lac-Mégantic disaster, the Transportation Safety Board released statistics on "uncontrolled movements of rolling stock" (cars and locomotives), more commonly called "runaways."[8] An accompanying statement from board chair Kathy Fox reminded the government of its failure to implement the board's post–Lac-Mégantic recommendation for additional protections against runaways, as well as its ongoing concerns with the vulnerability of older tank cars and Transport Canada's oversight of safety management systems.

The numbers, which compared the five years preceding 2013 with the four years following, were alarming: The average annual number of runaways jumped 21 per cent, from forty-eight to fifty-eight. Almost two-thirds of runaways over the entire period were caused by lack of securement. The percentage of runaways involving derailments climbed in the second period, as did the average annual number of incidents involving dangerous goods, climbing from eleven to fifteen.

Earlier in 2018, the Transportation Safety Board had reported 115 railway accidents in 2017 involving dangerous goods, including five in which contents spilled. This was up from one hundred dangerous goods accidents in 2016, of which two involved spills.[9] This comes at a time when Canadian oil-by-rail export volumes for June 2018 reached record levels.

All told, the numbers told a tale: The problem of runaways was itself a runaway.

Epilogue

As this book went to press, it had been more than five years since Gaston and Pauline Bégnoche's world fell apart on July 6, 2013.

Their daughter, Talitha Coumi Bégnoche, and their granddaughters, nine-year-old Bianka and four-year-old Alyssa, were asleep in their apartment a stone's throw from the railway tracks when they were consumed by an inferno of exploding oil.

The previous afternoon, Gaston had been sitting on a bench by Lac Mégantic with his daughter and granddaughters: playing, laughing, eating, discussing summer plans. They were the light of his life.

It was the last time he would see them.

In 2018, Gaston and Pauline are still grappling with the pain and anguish of their loss. Talitha's two sisters, Nadine and Karyne, are still grieving, trying to come to terms with the reality of their sister's death. The family's grief is mixed with anger that no one has been held accountable for taking away their loved ones.

Another forty-four people also died that night, their hopes and dreams obliterated, futures wiped out. Two more victims followed in suicides. Twenty-seven children lost their parents. Families lost their sons, daughters, mothers, fathers, brothers, sisters, cousins, aunts, uncles. Others lost their friends, lovers, fellow workers, classmates, teammates. No one in the town was spared the grief of their loss.

Their deaths were collateral damage from the culmination of decisions stretching back more than three decades. Mutually reinforcing policies of deregulation, privatization and fiscal austerity; power relationships that subordinated government's obligation to protect its citizens to the private interest of corporations; decisions that were driven by greed, corruption and hubris — all aligned that terrible night.

The tragedy is only deepened by the sorry fact, demonstrated in the preceding pages, that government has not taken appropriate steps to prevent another Lac-Mégantic.

The victims were remembered once again on the fifth anniversary of the tragedy, as they will continue to be remembered: with love and longing. They are:

Marie-Semie Alliance	Marie-Noëlle Faucher
Alyssa Charest Bégnoche	Jacques Giroux
Bianka Charest Bégnoche	Natachat Gaudreau
Talitha Coumi Bégnoche	Michel Junior Guertin
Diane Bizier	David Lacroix-Beaudoin
Guy Bolduc	Gaétan Lafontaine
Stéphane Bolduc	Karine Lafontaine
Yannick Bouchard	Stéphane Lapierre
Marie-France Boulet	Jo-Annie Lapointe
Yves Boulet	Henriette Latulippe
Frédéric Boutin	David Martin
Geneviève Breton	Roger Paquet
Karine Champagne	Éliane Parenteau-Boulanger
Sylvie Charron	Éric Pépin-Lajeunesse
Kathy Clusiault	Mathieu Pelletier
Réal Custeau	Louisette Poirier-Picard
Denise Dubois	Marianne Poulin
Maxime Dubois	Wilfrid Ratsch

Martin Rodrigue   Joanie Turmel
Jean-Pierre Roy   Lucie Vadnais
Kevin Roy   Jean-Guy Veilleux
Mélissa Roy   Richard Veilleux
Andrée-Anne Sévigny
Jimmy Sirois   Kevin Morin
Élodie Turcotte   Yvon Ricard

An essential part of the act of remembrance is not forgetting what happened, why it happened and who was responsible. This book has sought to shed light on these questions.

Susan Dodd lost her brother in the sinking of the Ocean Ranger oil rig off the coast of Newfoundland on February 15, 1982. In her book, *The Ocean Ranger: Remaking the Promise of Oil*, she warned: "Time and time again, publics trust governments to ensure that companies operate prudently. Time and again, we are shocked by a new disaster caused by corporate negligence. We say, 'We will never forget.' Then we forget. And then it happens again."

Let us not forget Lac-Mégantic.

Glossary

American Fuel & Petrochemical Manufacturers: A national U.S. trade association and lobby group representing 98 per cent of oil refining capacity in the US.

American Petroleum Institute: The largest national US trade association and lobby, representing companies in all facets of the oil and natural gas industry.

Association of American Railroads: The main US freight railroad trade lobby.

Burlington Northern Santa Fe: The largest freight railway, and largest shipper of crude by rail, in North America. It is a wholly owned subsidiary of Warren Buffett's private holding company, Berkshire Hathaway.

Business Council on National Issues: A big-business lobby comprised of the 150 largest corporations in Canada. Founded in 1976, it was renamed the Canadian Council of Chief Executives in 2001 and renamed the Business Council of Canada in 2016.

Cabinet Directive on Regulatory Management: The government-wide regulatory policy implemented by the Harper government in 2012.

Canadian Association of Petroleum Producers: The main lobby group for Canada's upstream conventional oil, oil sands and natural gas producers.

Canadian Rail Operating Rules: Introduced as part of the 1988 *Railway Safety Act*, they are for the most part drafted by the railways themselves, subject to approval by Transport Canada. They replaced various regulations and orders formerly implemented within Transport Canada.

Canadian Transportation Agency (formerly the National Transportation Agency): The federal agency responsible for economic regulations in the rail sector: issuing railway operating certificates, approving new railway lines and resolving disputes with the public and with other levels of government.

Central Maine & Quebec Railway: American railway company owned by Fortress Investments, which bought the assets of the bankrupt

Montreal, Maine and Atlantic Railway in 2014 and began operations shortly thereafter.

Canadian National Railway (CN): Originally a Crown corporation, it was formed in 1917 from the assets of multiple bankrupt private Canadian companies. Its passenger service was taken over by Via Rail in 1978. As a freight railway, it was privatized by the Liberal government in 1995. With an extensive network of tracks in Canada and the US, CN is one of the largest railway companies in North America. It carries coal and petroleum products, including bitumen.

Canadian Pacific Railway (CP): Incorporated in 1881 with the original purpose of building the transcontinental railway. Headquartered in Calgary, it has over 22,000 kilometres of track in Canada and the US, one of the largest networks in North America. It is a major carrier of oil by rail including from the Bakken region of North Dakota. In 2012–13, it transported Bakken crude to the Irving oil refinery in Saint John, New Brunswick. It subcontracted to Montreal, Maine and Atlantic Railway for a part of the trip through Quebec and Maine, including through Lac-Mégantic.

Coalition des Citoyens: A citizens watchdog group, one of several formed in Lac-Mégantic after the disaster. Its full name is: la Coalition des citoyens et organismes engagés pour la sécurité ferroviaire de Lac-Mégantic.

CPC-1232: A modestly strengthened version of the standard DOT-111 tank car model designed by the Association of American Railroads. It was in production from 2012 to 2015, until replaced by the TC/DOT-117.

Department of Transportation: The American federal cabinet department responsible for acts policies, regulations and programs for all modes of transportation.

Dilbit: Diluted bitumen. It is bitumen from the Alberta oil sands, diluted with a mixture of highly volatile liquids including benzene and naphtha, enabling it to be pumped easily into tank cars and pipelines. When bitumen is diluted by synthetic crude, the blend, also volatile, is called synbit.

DOT-111: A standard model of tank car used to carry flammable liquids and other dangerous goods such as crude oil. These tank cars derailed and spilled in Lac-Mégantic in 2013. They were completely eliminated from carrying crude oil in Canada in 2016.

Emergency response assistance plans: Plans required to be put in place by railway companies and approved by Transport Canada for the event of derailments involving trains carrying dangerous goods.

Energy Policy Institute of Canada: A not-for-profit organization comprised of Canada's largest petroleum corporations, established to advance their commercial interests.

Federal Energy Regulatory Commission: The US federal energy regulator.

Federal Railroad Administration: The agency within the US Department of Transportation responsible for railway safety.

Montreal, Maine and Atlantic Railway: An American-owned short-line railway company transporting Bakken crude oil through Quebec's Eastern Townships on its way to the Irving oil refinery in Saint John, New Brunswick, in 2012–13.

North American Free Trade Agreement (NAFTA): The trilateral trade and investment agreement between the United States, Canada and Mexico, implemented in 1994, and, as of 2018, under renegotiation.

National Research Council: The federal government's primary national research and technology body. Its mandate is to undertake, assist or promote scientific and industrial research.

National Transportation Safety Board: The American transportation accident investigation agency.

Pipeline and Hazardous Materials Safety Administration: Agency within the US Department of Transportation responsible for the transportation of dangerous goods.

PG I, PG II, PG III: Designations of class III flammable liquids ("PG" being short for packing group), which denote levels of volatility or degree of danger, with PG I being the highest-volatility liquid, and PG III the lowest-volatility liquid.

Prime Minister's Office: A partisan body comprised of top political staff chosen by the prime minister and not part of public service. The Prime Minister's Office serves the prime minister exclusively, providing partisan support and advice on policy and political priorities. It constitutes a link between decisions of the prime minister and the operation of government.

Privy Council Office: The top public service body. Led by the clerk of the Privy Council, it oversees the federal public service and provides non-partisan policy advice to the prime minister and cabinet. It is also responsible for executing the policy decisions made by the government.

Quebec North Shore and Labrador Railway: A freight railway in northern Quebec carrying mostly iron ore, the only company prior to Montreal, Maine and Atlantic Railway given permission to operate its trains with single-person crews, albeit with a large number of conditions.

Railway Association of Canada: Canada's main railway lobby, representing more than fifty freight and passenger railway companies, as well as a number of industrial railways and railway supply companies as associate members.

Railway Safety Act: Came into force in 1988. The primary law governing railway safety in Canada, it is implemented through regulations including those involving safety management systems — plans by which companies are required to manage their safety. It also initiated the Canadian Rail Operating Rules. The *Act* has been amended several times, most recently by the 2015 *Safe and Accountable Rail Act.*

Railway Safety Directorate: The body within Transport Canada responsible for regulating railway safety.

Railway Workers United: A US-based union, which advocates on behalf of railway workers in all professions, including locomotive engineers and conductors, in both Canada and the US.

Royal Society of Canada: The senior collegium of distinguished scholars, artists and scientists in the country. Its primary objective is to promote learning and research in the arts, humanities and the natural and social sciences. It also seeks to advise governments, non-governmental organizations and Canadians broadly speaking on matters of public interest.

Safety management systems: Introduced in 2001, these constitute the rail safety regulatory regime. Safety management systems are developed and managed by the rail companies themselves in accordance with regulatory criteria established by Transport Canada. Plans are overseen and audited by Transport Canada personnel.

Single-person train operations: Transport Canada granted permission to Montreal, Maine and Atlantic in 2012 to run its crude oil trains through Quebec's Eastern Townships with a single operator (i.e., locomotive engineer): the only company in Canada operating its oil trains in this manner.

Sûreté du Québec: Quebec's provincial police.

TC/DOT-117: the new, strengthened tank car model designed in the wake of Lac-Mégantic by Canadian and American governments for the transportation of flammable liquids including crude oil. Production of these cars and the retrofit of existing cars began in 2015 and will completely replace CPC-1232 model tank cars by 2025.

Synbit: See dilbit.

Teamsters Canada Rail Conference: Part of Teamsters Canada, represents sixty thousand workers in the rail industry, including CN and CP and most short-line railways in Canada.

Transport Canada: The department within the federal government responsible for all transportation-related acts, policies, regulations and programs. It employs about five thousand people at its Ottawa headquarters and in five regional offices across the country. It reports to the minister of transport.

Transportation of Dangerous Goods Act: The purpose of the 1992 *Transportation of Dangerous Goods Act* is to ensure the safe transport of dangerous goods in all modes of transport. The Act establishes all pertinent regulations as well as criminal penalties for violations of its provisions.

Transportation of Dangerous Goods Directorate: The body within Transport Canada responsible for regulating the transportation of dangerous goods.

Transportation Safety Board: The independent Canadian agency responsible for investigating transportation accidents and making recommendations to Transport Canada regarding safety improvements.

TSB Watchlist: The Transportation Safety Board's Watchlist identifies the key transportation safety issues that need to be addressed by Transport Canada.

Unifor: Canada's largest industrial union. It represents workers in the rail transportation sector including at CN and VIA Rail.

Unit oil train: A train carrying an uninterrupted chain of typically between 70 and 110 crude oil tank cars.

United Steelworkers Canada: Union that represented Montreal, Maine and Atlantic Railway workers and those of its successor, Central Maine & Quebec Railway.

Union of Canadian Transport Employees: A component of the Public Service Alliance Canada, representing a majority of Transport Canada and transportation agency employees.

Via Rail: The publicly owned passenger rail company (a Crown Corporation) formed in 1978, which took over the passenger services of CN, CP and several smaller railways.

Acknowledgements

My career as a policy analyst and executive director of the Canadian Centre for Policy Alternatives offered me a rare platform to offer a counterpoint to the official view on the Lac-Mégantic disaster.

In August 2013, I travelled to Lac-Mégantic with my son, Ryan, to witness the devastation. We wandered the town silently, trying to absorb the magnitude of the catastrophe.

On my return to Ottawa, I got a shock. My colleague Diane Touchette told me three members of her extended family had perished in the tragedy. Her cousin Pauline and Pauline's husband, Gaston, lost their daughter, Talitha Coumi Bégnoche, and their two granddaughters, four-year-old Alyssa and nine-year-old Bianka, in the inferno. I spent an emotional afternoon with Gaston and Pauline Bégnoche.

Ultimately, I would write three reports on the disaster. The first one, *Where Does the Buck Stop?*, was released in October 2013. Shortly thereafter, I got a call from Sylvie Fournier, a Radio-Canada journalist with the investigative program *Enquête*, wanting to meet. It was the beginning of an enduring friendship.

When I decided I would leave the Canadian Centre for Policy Alternatives at the end of 2015, my friend Elizabeth Sheehy, a law professor at the University of Ottawa, encouraged me to apply for a Law Foundation of Ontario Community Leadership in Justice Fellowship. I wish to express my profound gratitude to the law foundation for granting me this fellowship.

I spent 2016 at the University of Ottawa law faculty, continuing my research, giving lectures, conducting directed research courses, speaking at events outside the university and testifying before Parliament. I was warmly welcomed and supported by faculty members, including Sheehy, Jennifer Quaid, Heather McLeod-Kilmurray, Lynda Collins, David Robitaille, Viviana Fernandez, John Packer and Cintia Quiroga; as well by Steven Bittle (criminology) and Caroline Burgess (geography).

I am also grateful to the dedicated students I supervised — among them, Jasmine van Schouwen, Valerie Akujobi and Rachel Nadeau —

who contributed to my own understanding of the issues. Liette Gilbert and Mark Winfield of York University's Faculty of Environmental Studies likewise have been incredibly supportive of my work.

Christine Collins, president of the Union of Canadian Transportation Employees, and Brian Stevens, Unifor national rail director, supported my work, as did Fritz Edler from Railway Workers United.

In June 2016, I was invited to go to Lac-Mégantic by two local citizens groups to witness their meeting with the House of Commons Transport Committee. The core members are identified in the text. I am especially indebted to Robert Bellefleur, the Coalition des Citoyens spokesperson, who has generously shared with me his insights, knowledge and experience of the tragedy and its aftermath.

My year at the university culminated with a conference that brought to Ottawa for the first time Lac-Mégantic citizens group representatives to engage with politicians, media, policy analysts, rail safety experts, civil society activists and legal, economic and environmental scholars.

As my time at the university was drawing to an end, I debated whether I had more to contribute to the understanding of the tragedy. Jim Lorimer persuaded me that the story of Lac-Mégantic needed to reach a wider audience. Thus began the next stage of my journey, this book. I thank the Ontario Arts Council for financial assistance during its writing.

Writing a book is both a lonely experience and a collaborative endeavour. Along the way, I received feedback from Dean Beeby, Bellefleur, André Blais, Dodd, Alex Himelfarb, Ryan Campbell, Fournier, Harry Gow, Justin Mikulka, Stuart Trew, Gilbert and Winfield.

Gow generously shared his knowledge of all things railway. Geneviève Boulanger reviewed early drafts of several chapters and translated a summary. Ian Bron and John Dalziel shared their experiences in the marine transport sector.

I gained indispensable knowledge from interviews with independent railway experts and former government insiders, most of whom wish to remain anonymous. Those who agreed to be on record include Steve Callaghan, Jean-Pierre Gagnon and Kevin Mosher. I am deeply grateful to Steve Callaghan who shared with me his knowledge, opinions and insights based on fifty years of experience with the railways, as a Transportation Safety Board investigator, and as expert trial witness. None of these persons are to blame for any errors or omissions on my part.

I benefited immensely from the reporting of journalists who covered the Lac-Mégantic story. Many are referenced in the text.

I also learned from people who, like me, were inspired by the tragedy to produce intellectual and artistic works: Anaïs Valiquette L'Heureux's doctoral dissertation *La tragedie de Lac-Mégantic et l'atrophie de la vigilance dans le secteur public*; Anne-Marie Saint-Cerny's book *Mégantic*; Alexia Bürger's play *Les Hardings*; Len Falkenstein's play *Lac/Athabasca*; Jacques Rancourt's poem *Quarante-sept stations pour une ville dévastée*; photo exhibitions by Michel Huneault and Benoit Aquin; and finally my friend, the late Jeff Watson, a sculptor whose commissioned memorial piece, *Les Messagers*, resides in the Parc des veterans on the shore of Lac-Mégantic.

My thanks to Tom Harding's lawyers, Thomas Walsh and Charles Shearson; to my awesome former colleagues at the Canadian Centre for Policy Alternatives; to Guillaume Hébert and colleagues from the Institut de recherche et d'informations socio-économiques; to Jim Turk, director of the Ryerson University Centre for Free Expression; to Peter Northcote, currently with the New Zealand Transport Accident Investigation Commission; and to Patricia Lai and Helen Vassilakos, co-founders the Toronto-based citizens group Safe Rail Communities.

Thank you to Jim Lorimer and Carrie Gleason for believing in this project, and to the James Lorimer & Company Ltd., Publishers team, Sara D'Agostino and William Brown; and to my editor, Ted Mumford, who turned a cumbersome and somewhat disjointed manuscript into a tightly drawn narrative. He is quite simply the best.

And finally, I am beholden to my dear wife (and sometime translator), Nathalie Poirier, who has been by my side in unwavering support every step of the way.

Endnotes

CHAPTER 1

1. There is a large literature on regulatory capture, from the work of Chicago school economist George Stigler concerned with monopolies stifling competition, to more recent work focused on public interest issues: health, safety and the environment. Elizabeth Warren, "Corporate Capture of the Rulemaking Process," *Regulatory Review*, June 14, 2016; Jason MacLean, "Striking at the Root Problem of Canadian Environmental Law: Identifying and Escaping Regulatory Capture," *Journal of Environmental Law and Practice* 29 (February 23, 2016), 111–134; Amitai Etzioni,"The Capture Theory of Regulations—Revisited," *Society* 46, no. 4 (May 6, 2009), 319–323; Daniel Carpenter and David A. Moss, *Preventing Regulatory Capture: Special Interest Influence and How to Limit It* (Cambridge, UK: Cambridge University Press, 2013). On corporate power, see also: Joel Bakan, *The Corporation* (New York: Free Press, 2005), 150.
2. Anaïs Valiquette L'Heureux, "La tragédie du Lac-Mégantic et l'atrophie de la vigilance dans le secteur public," Thèse, École nationale d'administration publique.
3. Ibid., 212.
4. Ibid., 185.
5. Jasmine van Schouwen, "What Makes a Dangerous Goods Disaster? The Regulatory Perspective," *Revue générale de droit* 48 (2018): 177–226.
6. Susan Dodd, *The Ocean Ranger: Remaking the Promise of Oil* (Black Point, NS: Fernwood Publishing, 2012).
7. Steven Bittle, *Still Dying for a Living: Corporate Criminal Liability after the Westray Mine Disaster* (Vancouver: UBC Press, 2013).
8. Mark Winfield, *Blue-Green Province: The Environment and the Political Economy of Ontario* (Vancouver: UBC Press, 2012).
9. Ken Hatt and Kierstin Hatt, "Neoliberalizing Food Safety and the 2008 Canadian Listeriosis Outbreak," *Agriculture and Human Values* 29, no. 1 (2012): 17–28.
10. For this and other insights into patterns common to major disasters I'm indebted to the work of Susan Dodd, *Ocean Ranger*.

CHAPTER 2

1. In 2011, the loan was fully paid back by Montreal, Maine and Atlantic Railway. Its equity interest in the company, which represented 13 per cent of total equity capital, was worth only $1,000 by the end of December 2012.
2. Nick Sambides, Jr., "Montréal Maine & Atlantic Railway Railway Using Remote Control," *Bangor Daily News*, May 28, 2010, updated January 29, 2011.
3. Julian Sher, "Lac Megantic: Railway's History of Cost-Cutting," *Toronto Star*, July 11, 2013.
4. L'Heureux, "Tragedie du Lac-Mégantic," 137.
5. Ibid., 183.
6. Canada, Treasury Board Secretariat, *Cabinet Directive on Streamlining Regulation* (Her Majesty the Queen in Right of Canada, Cat No BT22-110/2007). A paper commissioned by the External Advisory Committee on Smart Regulation (EACSR) to assess public opinion concluded that government must be in the driver's seat: "From a

citizen's perspective, it is unrealistic to expect industry to self-regulate its behaviour so as to ensure a safe environment and protect the country's natural resources. And the same argument was applied to the companies that produce pharmaceuticals and other health products and services." Leslie Pal, Judith Maxwell, "Assessing the Public Interest in the 21st Century: A Framework," prepared for the External Advisory Committee on Smart Regulation, January 2004.

7.   Royal Society of Canada, "Elements of Precaution: Recommendations for the Regulation of Food Biotechnology in Canada," January 2001.

CHAPTER 3

1.   Kevin Taft, *Oil's Deep State: How the Petroleum Industry Undermines Democracy and Stops Action on Global Warming – in Alberta, and in Ottawa* (Toronto: James Lorimer & Co., 2017).

2.   Bruce Campbell, *The Petro-Path Not Taken* (Ottawa: Canadian Centre for Policy Alternatives, January 2013).

3.   Ibid.

4.   Andrew Nikiforuk, *Slick Water* (Vancouver: Greystone books, 2015), 224.

5.   Taft, *Oil's Deep State*, 22–40.

6.   Union of Canadian Transportation Employees, *Canada's Broken Transportation Oversight System, a Concerned Inspectorate Speaks: Recommendations for Reforms to Canada's Transportation Safety Regime*, 2014.

7.   Transportation Safety Board, *Railway Investigation Report R13D0054* (Gatineau, QC: 2014), 58–59, 99–105.

8.   Transportation Safety Board, advisory letter, July 18, 2013.

9.   Transportation Safety Board, advisory letter, July 8, 2013.

10.   The loophole was *General Rule M*; it read as follows: "Wherever the following: engine, train, transfer or movement appear in these rules, special instructions or general operating instructions, the necessary action will be carried out by a crew member or crew members of the movement. In addition: (i) Where only one crew member is employed, operating rules and instructions requiring joint compliance may be carried out by either the locomotive engineer or conductor, and (ii) in the absence of a locomotive engineer on a crew consisting of at least two members, the conductor will designate another qualified employee to perform the rules required duties of the locomotive engineer."

11.   Interview with the *Hill Times*, June 23, 2014.

12.   Canada Safety Council, "Improving Railway Safety," www.tc.gc.ca/media/documents/rsa-lsf/CSC.pdf.

13.   Transport Canada, *Stronger Ties: a Shared Commitment to Railway Safety* (Ottawa, Railway Safety Act Review Secretariat, 2007).

14.   E. Wayne Benedict, "Canada's Railway Safety Regulatory Regime: Past, Present and Future," *Transportation Law Journal* 34, no. 2 (2007): 147–165.

15.   Ibid., 164. The cities cited refer to the location of previous major railway accidents.

16.   Ibid., 164–65.

CHAPTER 4

1.   Grant Robertson and Jackie McNish, "Inside the Oil-Shipping Free-For-All That Brought Disaster to Lac-Mégantic," *Globe and Mail*, December 2, 2013. See also Grant Robertson and Jackie McNish, "How a Flawed Pipeline on Wheels Brought Disaster," *Globe and Mail*, December 3, 2013.

2. *North Dakota: The Next Hazardous Materials Frontier*, cited http://msnbcmedia.msn. com/i/MSNBC/Sections/NEWS/140115_Bakken_Inspection_.pdf.

3. David Thomas, "Federal hazmat regulator AWOL from North Dakota oilfields," *Railway Age*, November 10, 2015.

4. Transportation Safety Board, *Railway Investigation Report R13D0054*, 48.

CHAPTER 5

1. Chris Sorensen and Kate Lunau, "How Suspect Practices and Policies Helped Fuel the Lac-Mégantic Crash," *Maclean's*, July 12, 2013.

2. "Identification and evaluation of risk-mitigating countermeasures for single-person train operation," National Research Council Canada, Centre for Surface Transportation Technology, prepared for Transportation Technology and Innovation Directorate Policy Group, Project 54-R0193, Technical Report, March 2012.

CHAPTER 6

1. Red Tape Reduction Commission, "Why Cutting Red Tape Matters," www. reduceredtape.gc.ca/about-apropos/why-pourquoi-eng.asp

2. Canada, *Cabinet Directive on Regulatory Management* (2012), www.tbs-sct.gc.ca/ hgw-cgf/priorities-priorites/rtrap-parfa/guides/cdrm-dcgr-eng.asp. The policy was embedded in legislation with the 2015 *Red Tape Reduction Act* (Bill 21).

3. See for example this global review of voluntary guidelines: D. McCarthy and P. Morling, *Using Regulation as a Last Resort? Assessing the Performance of Voluntary Approaches* (Sandy, Bedfordshire, UK: Royal Society for the Protection of Birds, 2015), www.rspb.org.uk/Images/usingregulation_tcm9-408677.pdf.

4. Marc Lee, *Canada's Regulatory Obstacle Course* (Ottawa: Canadian Centre for Policy Alternatives, 2010).

5. Michael Harris, *Party of One: Stephen Harper and Canada's Radical Makeover* (Toronto: Viking, 2014), 421. The Harper government's efforts to muzzle scientists, control the bureaucracy and suppress information are documented in: Mark Bourrie, *Kill the Messengers* (Toronto: HarperCollins, 2015).

6. John Read, "What's in a Word?" Canadian Government Executive, January 24, 2014.

7. Obtained under Access to Information; Memorandum to minister, prepared by Transport Canada policy group, for Ed Fast Trade Minister and Dennis Lebel, Transport Minister, ATIP file number, A– 2013- 00004 – JD.

8. obtained under Access to Information; Memorandum to Minister, prepared by Transport Canada policy group; to Minister Ed fast [Trade] and Minister Joe Oliver[NRCAN]; ATIP file number, A– 2013- 00004 – JD.

9. Transport Canada, *Report on Plans and Priorities*, 2009–10, 2012–13, and 2013–14.

10. *Report and Recommendations of the Transportation of Dangerous Goods General Policy Advisory Council (GPAC) Emergency Response Assistance Plan (ERAP) Working Group*, January 31, 2014, 14.

11. Testimony, November 27, 2013.

12. Mike De Souza, "Transport Canada Safety Record Back Under Microscope Following Ottawa Crash," Canada.com, posted on September 18, 2013.

13. Ibid., 56.

14. *2011 December Report of the Comissioner of Environment and Sustainable Development*, www.oag-bvg.gc.ca/internet/English/parl_cesd_201112_e_36027.html

15. Mike De Souza, "Watchdogs Contradict Transport Canada Safety Oversight Claims Following Lac-Mégantic Disaster," *Postmedia News*, July 12, 2013.

16. Transportation Safety Board, *Railway Investigation Report R13D0054*, 82.
17. Jang-Shup Shin, *The Subversion of Shareholder Democracy and the Rise of Hedge-fund activism*, Working Paper, Institute for New Economic Thinking, August 2018.
18. Jesse Snyder, "The No Bullshit Legacy of Hunter Harrison," *Alberta Venture*, April 2017.
19. Gary Park , "The Nub of Lac-Mégantic," *Petroleum News Bakken*, July 13, 2013.
20. Eric Atkins, "Canadian Pacific Railway: The Cost of Success," *Globe and Mail*, March 4, 2017.
21. Cited Kristine Owram, "The Other Side of Hunter Harrison's CP Legacy," *Financial Post*, February 16, 2017.
22. Bruce E. Kelly, "It Shouldn't Take a $300 Million Man," *Railway Age*, March 27, 2017.
23. David Macdonald, "Climbing Up and Kicking Down: Executive Pay in Canada," Canadian Centre for Policy Alternatives, January 2018, 17.

CHAPTER 7

1. The director general of the Transportation of Dangerous Goods Directorate confirmed this in testimony before the House of Commons Transport Committee, November 27, 2013.
2. Author's calculation.
3. See Lobby Register: https://oclcal.gc.ca/app/secure/orl/lrrs/do/vwRg?cno=14798&regId =761815#regStart.

    Also cited in Linda Gyulai, "Railways Have Been Lobbying against More Stringent Safety Regulations," *Montreal Gazette*, July 13, 2013. www.montrealgazette.com/news/ railways+have+been+lobbying+against+more+stringent+safety+regulations/ 8654175/story.html.

    In its more recent submission, it changed the wording of its activity, removing the line assuring that current regulations regarding the transport of dangerous goods are sufficient. It reads as follows: "To inform about the movement of dangerous goods, including voluntary and regulatory requirements, volumes, customers, rail operators (Class 1, local and regional railways), safety measures and safety training to ensure regulations for dangerous goods transportation is adequate and conducive to safe railway operations." https://lobbycanada.gc.ca/app/secure/ocl-cal.gc.ca/app /secure/orl/lrrs/do/vwRg?cno=14798&regId=764948.
4. Testimony, May 23, 2013, cited, Senate Committee on Energy, Environment and Natural Resources, *Moving Energy Safely*, August 2013, 38.
5. John Nicol and Dave Seglins, "Just Before Lac-Mégantic, Railways Sought to Reduce Inspections," *CBC News*, February 4, 2014.
6. Kim Mackrael, "How Bakken Crude Moved from North Dakota to Lac-Mégantic," *Globe and Mail*, July 8, 2014.
7. Transportation Safety Board, *Railway Investigation Report R13D0054*, 104–5.
8. This chapter was written with the help of recordings released by the criminal investigation, witness testimony at the trial, findings of the Transportation Safety Board's Lac- Mégantic investigation report, personal communications with survivors and experts, and media reports and interviews.

CHAPTER 8

1. My account of what happened from the moment the train crashed into the centre of town and the days that followed is reconstructed from numerous sources: my own conversations with survivors, residents and investigators; audio recordings released by the police investigation; witness testimony at the trial; and accounts by various media

outlets including Radio-Canada, TVA Nouvelles, *La Presse, La Tribune, Toronto Star, Globe and Mail,* Canadian Press, *Le Journal de Montréal* and *Le Devoir.*

CHAPTER 9

1. Mike De Souza, "PM Says Rules 'Not Abided By' in Disaster at Lac-Megantic," *Postmedia News,* December 6, 2013.
2. Kevin Quigley et al., *Too Critical To Fail: How Canada Manages Threats to Critical Infrastructure* (Montreal: McGill-Queens University Press, 2017), 239–40.
3. Jacquie McNish and Grant Robertson, "The Deadly Secret Behind the Lac-Mégantic Inferno," *Globe and Mail,* December 3, 2013.
4. Government of Canada, *Canada-United States Regulatory Cooperation Council Joint Forward Plan,* August 29, 2014, http://publications.gc.ca/collections/collection_2014/sct-tbs/BT22-126-2014-eng.pdf.
5. Cited in Jessica Barrett, "Rail Transport of Hazardous Goods in Canada is 'Safe', Says Federal Government," *Postmedia News,* January 13, 2014. Data from the US Pipeline and Hazardous Materials Safety Administration recorded almost twice as much oil spilled from derailments in 2013 than the total for the forty years ending in 2012.
6. "Railway Operating Certificate Regulations," *Canada Gazette* 148, no. 24 (November 19, 2014), www.gazette.gc.ca/rp-pr/p2/2014/2014-11-19/html/sor-dors258-eng.php.
7. John Nicol and Dave Seglins, "Rail Companies Fight New Rules to Prevent Crew Fatigue," *CBC News,* October 8, 2014, www.cbc.ca/news/canada/rail-companies-fight-new-rules-to-prevent-crew-fatigue-1.2785581.
8. *InsideClimate News* and the Weather Channel, in partnership with the Investigative Fund at the Nation Institute.

CHAPTER 10

1. Opening remarks from Wendy Tadros, Transportation Safety Board chair, on the release of *Railway Investigation Report R13D0054,* August 19, 2014, www.bst-tsb.gc.ca/eng/medias-media/discours-speeches/2014/08/20140819.asp.
2. Transportation Safety Board, *Railway Investigation Report R13D0054,* 130, www.tsb.gc.ca/eng/rapports-reports/rail/2013/r13d0054/r13d0054.asp.
3. Transportation Safety Board Report, *Railway Investigation Report R09T0057* (February 11, 2009).
4. Personal communication.
5. Hadar Rosenhand, Emilie Roth and Jordan Multer, *Cognitive and Collaborative Demands of Freight Conductor Activities: Results and Implications of a Cognitive Task Analysis* (Washington, DC: Federal Railroad Administration, July 2012).
6. Don Mustard, conference presentation, *Lac-Mégantic, Oh, mon Dieu;* cited Greg Meckbach, *Federal investigator discusses Lac-Megantic at Engineering Insurance Conference,* Canadian Underwriter for October 9, 2015.

CHAPTER 11

1. Accessed at: www.rsc-src.ca/en/about-us/our-people/our-priorities/expert-panel-report-•-behaviour-and-environmental-impacts-crude.
2. Allison Martell, "CN Rail Struggled with Track Improvements after Fiery Derailments," *Reuters,* April 29, 2016.
3. Justin Mikulka, "Wild West approach to regulation in the Bakken shale means bomb trains continue to roll," *Desmog,* October 7, 2014.
4. Justin Mikulka, "66 singing industry's tune, how Jeff Denham's plans to delay oil by rail safety improvements," *Desmog,* February 12, 2015.

CHAPTER 12

1. Sylvie Fournier, "Le vautour de Lac-Mégantic," *Enquête*, Radio-Canada, March 20, 2017.
2. Cited: Allan Woods, "Federal Government Named in Lac-Mégantic Class-Action Lawsuit," *Toronto Star*, February 13, 2014.
3. Andy Blatchford, "Feds Paid $75M Settlement for Lac-Megantic Victims to Avoid Lawsuits," *Canadian Press*, May 2, 2016.
4. Associated Press, "Lawyer for Families of Train Derailment Victims to Sue Canadian Railroad," October 14, 2015.
5. Jennifer Brown, "CP to Challenge CCAA Jurisdiction Issue in Lac-Mégantic Settlement," *Canadian Lawyer*, June 8, 2015.
6. Eric Atkins, "CP Rail Denies Fault in Lac-Mégantic Disaster," *Globe and Mail*, June 2, 2017.

CHAPTER 13

1. Alexandre Robillard, "Lac-Mégantic: Amir Khadir choqué par le «cirque» de la comparution," *La Presse*, May 14, 2014.
2. Harry Glasbeek, *Class Privilege: How Law Shelters Shareholders and Coddles Capitalism* (Toronto: Between the Lines, 2017), 133.
3. Personal communication with author.
4. Glasbeek, *Class Privilege*, 167.
5. Ibid., 302.
6. The Swiss cheese model of accident causation was originally formulated by James Reason. "The Contribution of Latent Human Failures to the Breakdown of Complex Systems," *Philosophical Transactions of the Royal Society of London, Series B, Biological Sciences* 327, no. 1241 (1990): 475–484.

CHAPTER 14

1. Mélissa Généreux et al., "The Public Health Response during and after the Lac-Mégantic Train Derailment Tragedy," *Disaster Health* 2, no. 3–4 (2014): 113–120; Mélissa Généreux et al., The Public Health Response during and after the Lac-Mégantic Train Derailment Disaster," *European Journal of Public Health* 26, suppl. 1 (November 1, 2016); "Plus de trois ans après la tragédie : comment la communauté du Granit se porte-t-elle?" *Bulletin Vision Santé Publique* 34 (janvier 2017).
2. Ana de Santiago-Martin et. al., "Oil Spill in Lac-Mégantic, Canada: Environmental Monitoring and Remediation," *International Journal of Water and Wastewater Treatment* 2, no. 1 (January 2016).
3. Two early citizens groups were Sécu-Rail and le Comité citoyen de la region de Lac-Mégantic.
4. My primary relationship has been with the Coalition des Citoyens. My understanding of events in the five years since the tragedy has also been enhanced by the reporting and commentary in the local newspaper, *L'Écho de Frontenac*, and its editor Remi Tremblay; by Ronald Martel, a reporter for *La Presse*; and by Jonathan Santerre, whose Carré Bleu Facebook page has provided an invaluable archive of information. None of the above-mentioned individuals bear responsibility for any errors, omissions or other faux pas I may have committed.
5. Jacques Gagnon first contacted me as a member of another citizens group: La Comité de vigilance pour la sécurité ferroviaire de Lac-Mégantic.
6. Liette Gilbert, "The Crisis After the Crisis: Neoliberalized Discourses of Urgency, Risk

and Resilience in the Reconstruction of Lac-Mégantic," in "Have the Lessons of the Lac-Mégantic Rail Disaster Been Learned?" special issue, *Revue générale de droit* 48 (2018).

CHAPTER 15

1. Jennifer Winter, "Safety in numbers: Evaluating Canadian rail safety data," University Of Calgary: School of Public Policy, *SPP Communiqué* 6, no. 2 (April 2014).
2. Cited in Carol Linnitt, "Federal Freedom of Information in Canada Worse Now Than Under Harper: New Report," *Narwhal*, September 29, 2017.
3. Justin Mikulka, "Trump's New Era of Industry Self-Regulation Begins for Oil by Rail," *DeSmog*, May 11, 2017.
4. Justin Mikulka, "Federal Railroad Administration Nominee Plans to Push Rail Industry to Self-Regulate," *DeSmog Canada*, September 29, 2017.
5. Dawn Gagnon, "Railway Leaders Reflect on Progress Made in Rebuilding Line," *Bangor Daily News*, February 15, 2016.
6. Darren Fishell, "Firm That Bought Bankrupt Railway after Lac-Mégantic Tragedy Reports 2016 Profit," *Bangor Daily News*, February 28, 2017.
7. Brett Owens, "Three 7%–9% Yielders That Can Grow by 10% or More," *Forbes*, December 17, 2017, www.forbes.com/sites/brettowens/2017/12/17/three-7-9-yielders-that-can-grow-by-10-or-more/#5987d4bb577c.
8. Transportation Safety Board, "Uncontrolled Movement of Rolling Stock Related to Transportation Safety Board Investigation Report (R16T0111)," Backgrounder, June 27, 2018, www.tsb.gc.ca/eng/medias-media/fiches-facts/r16t0111/r16t0111-20180627-03.asp.
9. Levi Garber, "Jump in Serious Rail, Pipeline Accidents in 2017," *Canadian Press*, February 22, 2018.

Index